D1017020

Who Killed
Virginia Woolf?

Sculpture by Alma Bond
Photograph by Alcindor

Who Killed Virginia Woolf?

A Psychobiography

Alma Halbert Bond, Ph.D.

INSIGHT BOOKS
HUMAN SCIENCES PRESS, INC.

Library of Congress Cataloging in Publication Data

Bond, Alma Halbert.
  Who Killed Virginia Woolf?

   Bibliography: p.
   Includes index.
     1. Woolf, Virginia, 1882–1941—Biography—Psychology.
   2. Novelists, English—20th century—Biography.
   3. Psychoanalysis and literature. I. Title.
   PR6045.072Z5614 1989   823'.912 [B]   87-35710
   ISBN 0-89885-427-X

This book is dedicated to
Zane, Janet, and Jonathan,
Who are everything children should be
But rarely are.

Contents

List of Illustrations

Acknowledgments

This book had its beginning in a dream years ago. In it a voice directed me to go to Saint Ives and enter Tolland House, the home where Virginia Woolf spent so many of her early ecstatic summers. I went to Saint Ives, entered the "house" of Virginia Woolf, and shortly thereafter began this book.

I am indebted to the art of psychoanalysis for helping me to see with a deeper eye. Early in my professional career, I had another dream which determined my subsequent path. I dreamed that Freud and his colleagues were surrounded by a great magnetic force which lifted me off the ground until I was as tall as they. Psychoanalysis has indeed lifted me to greater heights than I could ever have dreamed of, for instance to writing the psychobiography of Virginia Woolf.

To help accomplish this, many friends, colleagues, relatives, and patients have shared their hard-won insights, as well as the generous gift of time. Dr. Gladys Natchez, my friend, colleague, and first editor, has always been available to explore ideas, offer encouragement, and read and discuss my chapters as they rolled off the computer. Words cannot give adequate credit for her con-

The author at Talland House

tribution. I am also grateful, although not at the time, for the sharp scalpel with which she cut this book.

I wish to thank my friends and colleagues, Doctors Margaret Ray, Daisy Franco, and Arlene Kramer Richards, my sister, Mrs. Pauline Stein, and my niece, Susan Stein, for their immensely valuable critiques of my first draft. Special thanks and appreciation also go to Dr. Ray for her beautiful photographs of the flowers shown in Chapter 1, her excellent and industrious work in transferring my photographs to slides, and for her enduring friendship the whole of our professional lives. I am also grateful to Mickey Ordover, Peggy L. Kerr, and Gladys Nussenbaum for their helpful suggestions. I would also like to express my thanks to Joe Henson for my portrait, and to Alcindor for the photo of my sculpture of Virginia Woolf.

I am indebted to Ms. Norma Fox, vice-president and editor-in-chief of Human Sciences Press, who believed in this book from the moment my first query crossed her desk. I am fortunate indeed to have found her for my first book.

I wish to thank my son Zane for his determination to help market the book, my daughter Janet for her constant encouragement and interest, and, especially, my son Jonathan, the "whiz kid of Madison Avenue," for his extensive help in advertising the book. I am grateful to all three and to my late husband, Rudy Bond, for their good-humored tolerance and affection during the many years of arduous involvement in its research and writing.

A special mention to Dr. Beverly Schlack Randles, known to my family as the "Virginia Woolf lady," for introducing me to the wonderful world of Virginia Woolf in her course years ago at Marymount College.

I am indebted to my parent organization, the Institute for Psychoanalytic Training and Research, who have always allowed me to be a maverick within the framework of psychoanalysis, and whose enthusiastic response to my Virginia Woolf papers was inspirational.

I am grateful to Dr. Barry Panter, who twice invited me to speak on Virginia Woolf to appreciative audiences of the American Medical Education at conferences in Hawaii.

I am thankful to the *Journal of the American Academy of Psychoanalysis* for first recognizing the value of and publishing my articles on Virginia Woolf. Some of the material in Chapters 1 and 2 originally appeared in these articles under the titles *Virginia Woolf: Manic-depressive Psychosis and Genius. An Illustration of Separation-Individuation Theory,* and *Virginia Woolf and Leslie Stephen: A Father's Contribution to Psychosis and Genius* (Copyright John Wiley & Sons, Inc.).

The author further acknowledges with gratitude permission to reprint material from the following sources:

Basic Books, Inc. for material from *The Psychological Birth of the Human Infant,* by Mahler, Pine, and Bergman, copyright 1975 by Margaret S. Mahler; Hoeber Medical Division, Harper & Row, for material from *Depression—Clinical, Experimental, and Theoretical Aspects,* by Aaron T. Beck, copyright 1967 by Aaron T. Beck; Harcourt, Brace and Jovanovich for material from *Virginia Woolf, Women and Writing,* by Virginia Woolf, copyright 1979 by Quentin Bell and Angelica Garnett; Random House for material from *Leslie Stephen, the Godless Victorian,* by Noel An-

Introduction

Who killed Virginia Woolf? What drove her over the brink when so many others were able to survive those difficult years? Who, if anyone, was chiefly responsible, when at the age of fifty-nine years and two months she made her way across the water meadows to the river *Ouse*, forced a large stone into the pocket of her coat, and threw herself into the river? The actual facts of her final years are now old history, and many accounts have been given by those supposedly closest to her, "explaining" her death (see Nigel Nicolson, 1900, pp. xv–xvii; Leonard Woolf, 1969, pp. 86–94, etc). But numerous biographical accounts, as well as Woolf's own prolific novels, diaries, and letters, serve to bury the real story under an avalanche of words. It is my contention that the multiple motivations for her suicide were far more covert than is suspected, and that we deliberately have been kept from understanding the dynamics as surely as the true paternity of Angelica Bell was kept secret from the world for many years (Garnett, 1985).

As a result of this widespread duplicity, despite the cascading proliferation of books and essays on her works and life we do not really understand Virginia Woolf. I believe that the only means of uncovering the truth at this late date is through a careful psychoanalytic study of her history and productions in which we regard her writing much as we do the free associations of the patient on the couch. Then, if we are fortunate, we may be the "voice that speaks fresh and strong" that Woolf despaired of ever finding.

Virginia herself was instrumental in colluding to keep the public, those she cared about, and probably even herself from facing the truth about her relationships. Perhaps the best way to discover what Virginia wished to keep secret is to compare the original drafts of her books with the published edition, as has been done so brilliantly by Mitchell A. Leaska, in *Pointz Hall* (1983). For example, the final version of *Between the Acts* (Woolf, 1941), which has been called "the longest suicide note in history," has been changed enough from its original draft to present an entirely different psychology of the relationship of the marital couple, Isa and Giles. The following passage of the second draft includes this paragraph, later to be deleted: "Then, the rage which they [the couple] had suppressed all day burst out. It was their part to tear each other asunder, to fight." "Virginia Woolf had indeed succeeded in suppressing the ferocity of her original plan," Leaska states. "At what price, however, only she would finally know." Since emotional honesty is the prime requisite for a true work of art, Virginia's "psychological tampering" with the book may well explain why she disliked the finished product, the writing of which "strained her" (Woolf, 1985, p. 290), to the point where she requested only a few days before her death that it be returned to her unpublished.

In the book, Giles has an affair with Mrs. Manresa. When Isa sees Giles welcoming the approaching Manresa, "who has him in thrall," Isa picks up a knife and wants to kill herself. " 'Plunge blade!' she said. And struck. 'Faithless!' she cried. Knife, too! It broke. So too my heart" (pp. 112–113). Later in the book, the impulse to murder herself instead of her husband has receded. Now Isa merely wants to end her pain through death. "Oh that our human pain could here have ending! . . . Oh that my life could here have ending, Isa murmured (taking care not to move her lips). Readily would she endow this voice with all her treasure if so be tears could be ended" (p. 181). By the final version of the manuscript, the reaction of Isa to her husband's betrayal with Manresa has changed even further from rageful anger to a benign attempt at reconciliation, presumably to protect the feelings of Virginia's own husband, Leonard. According to Leaska (p. 464), however, the disguise was incomplete, for as late as one month before her death Virginia worried that "something about it [the book] was wrong. She must erase from its pages certain irregularities of indictment, tone down her dangerous toying with people's names. She had played too many verbal tricks, swept in allusions too easily traceable."

Woolf's first title for *The Years* was *The Pargiters*. To parget, according to Webster (1969), means "to cover with plaster, to ornament with parge work." Virginia herself was the pargeter of her own truth. As early as 1923, she wrote in her diary (*A Writer's Diary*, 1953): "L. on the telephone expressed displeasure. Late again . . . I had no courage to venture against his will. Then I react. Of course it's a difficult question. For undoubtedly I get headaches or the jump in my heart; and then this spoils his pleasure. . . ." This emotional dishonesty went on throughout the marriage, to the extent of scapegoating Virginia's half-brothers as the individuals most responsible for her frigidity. During the time Virginia was writing *Between the Acts,* she was also rewriting *Lapin and Lapinova,* the story of a failed marriage, which she had put aside 20 years before, and had not picked up again until after the disillusionment with Leonard occurred that is postulated in Chapter 3.

Psychoanalysts often see patients suffering from a "family myth," in which a distorted view of the family is protected by all members in order to allow the family to function. Usually, in cases of this type, one member of the family is idealized, while another is scapegoated. In the Stephen family, the mother was the "angel in the house" (Woolf, 1967, p. 285) whom Virginia felt she had to "kill" in herself, in order to be able to write. In the Woolf family, it was Leonard who was the "angel." I believe that those who were in a position to know the truth needed to maintain the Woolf-Bell myth so that the family as a whole could go about their lives. In order to do this, Virginia's insanity had to be contained. Even her nephew, Quentin Bell, states (1972, Vol. 2, p. 18): "Her insanity was clothed, like some other painful things in that family, in a jest" with remarks such as "Oh you know very well the Goat's mad.'' They contained her madness largely by exalting Leonard as her caretaker, and rewarded him with membership in Bloomsbury, the most brilliant intellectual and social circle of our century.

This stratagem enabled Vanessa in particular to escape responsibility for her sister, and to reject Virginia at the times she needed Vanessa the most. For example, Quentin Bell (as quoted by Kushen, 1983, p. 40) argues that Vanessa's apparent indifference aggravated Virginia's grief, which culminated a few months later in her first serious breakdown. Vanessa, herself, had many problems to overcome. Nevertheless, she could have done a great deal more for Virginia but, for reasons of her own, chose not to.

To keep up the family myth, and enable the rest of the family to go about their lives in a relatively guilt-free manner, they found it necessary to deny difficulties in the Woolf marriage which were severe enough to force Virginia to seek the love of her life outside her marriage in a homosexual liaison with Vita Sackville-West.

By perpetuating the Woolf-Bell veil of secrecy with careful editing, withheld letters, a medley of partial truths, and a biased account of facts, the family has ensured that the public, too, has been taken in. As a result, the true story of Virginia's life and suicide, as well as the homosexual nature of her relationship with Vita Sackville-West, has been shrouded in silence. As Virginia wrote in an unpaginated, previously unpublished holograph entitled *Possible Poems* (Leaska, 1983, p. 504), "But none says what we can hear, none says what we believe, there's no voice that speaks fresh and strong, single & articulate, unspotted with damp, . . . always with corrupt murmurs. . . . '' That Virginia, herself, was not completely free of "corrupt murmurs" makes her statement more rather than less truthful.

Surely one of the most ironic statements of all time must be Virginia's letter to Vita (Woolf, 1977, p. 221) in which she states that these two women, who rejected sex with their husbands and found it necessary to go outside of marriage for their sexual gratification, were "in all London . . . alone like being married.'' In similar vein was the opening sentence in her suicide letter to Leonard (1980, p. 486), just before she took her last walk into the river: "I want to tell you that you have given me complete happiness.''

Leonard Woolf (1969, pp. 9–96) perpetuates the notion that it was the fear of madness that drove Virginia to her death. If so, and I do believe that fear is one factor to be considered, nobody has explained to my satisfaction what brought on that last attack. Bell implies (1972, pp. 211–226) that it was the uncertainties of the war that made Virginia kill herself. If so, and again, I believe the war was indeed one of the precipitating factors in her last illness, we must ask why Virginia was driven over the brink when so many others including Leonard himself were able to survive.

Virginia Woolf was not an integrated individual. She labored all her life to consolidate her personality, with only temporary success. In *Between the Acts,* she made a final heroic attempt to accomplish this difficult psychological task. But here again she failed. "Splintered," said Isa, finding the word for reflections in a looking-glass. "Shivered, splintered, fissured . . . dispersed are we. Desiring to be one, she was many" (Leaska, 1983, p. 181).

In my opinion, there was one means left to Virginia to unite her discordant selves: In her death she discovered the way to integrate the "orts, scraps, and fragments" (Woolf, 1941, p. 215) of her splintered soul. Then at last the important strains of her life—including the untimely disruption of the symbiosis with her mother and her early loss again through death, the highly ambivalent relationship with her father, the sadomasochistic interaction with her sister Vanessa, the loss of Vita as her lover, Virginia's disillusionment with Leonard and the "puncturing" of the family myth, the frightful experience of the war in the light of her inability to deal with aggression, and the death of Thoby and many of her friends, which reenacted the early traumatic deaths of her adolescence—all intermingled to culminate in her final act at the river Ouse. This book will attempt to examine these varied strains which ended her life so tragically, to show the contribution of each important player in her history toward both her genius and pathology, and to illustrate how all these strains coalesced to form the only possible ending to the life of Virginia Woolf.

1

Julia Stephen

"The Base upon Which Life Stands"

Virginia Woolf, one of the greatest women writers who ever lived, was diagnosed as a manic-depressive by physicians and family alike (Bell, 1972). She suffered at least four major psychotic breakdowns in her lifetime and took her own life by drowning at the age of fifty-nine. According to Wolf and Wolf (1979, p. 38), "There has been relatively little psychoanalytic interest in either Virginia Woolf or her oeuvre, to judge by the scarcity of references in the psychoanalytic literature." This study is an attempt to understand through the use of psychoanalytic methods some of the sources of her genius as well as the pathology that led to her breakdowns and suicide. Virginia Woolf will be our patient. Her works will be regarded much as an analysand's free associations. By this and other means the author-psychoanalyst will explore the depths of Virginia Woolf's unconscious so as to reveal her secret selves. In this way readers will be brought into the deep and exciting world of psychoanalysis along with Virginia Woolf.

Manic depression, or the bipolar disorder, is an illness in which the individual experiences affect changes ranging from boundless happiness to the depths of dejected desperation. In some cases, the moodswings are light enough to be integrated into a normal life-style, with only a slight exaggeration of highs and lows. In the extreme, the simplest functions of everyday life cannot be carried out and the individual must be hospitalized to preserve himself. Virginia Woolf is an example of the most severe form of the illness. She experienced extremes of high and low that required round-the-clock care of four nurses during her most acute phases, and the protective care of her husband Leonard even when she was comparatively well. The disease earned her the title of "The Invalid Lady of Bloomsbury" (Rose, 1978, xi).

The manic phase of this psychosis is characterized by a euphoric, unstable mood, psychomotor overactivity including sleeplessness, incessant motion, restlessness and agitation, and an increase in speed of thinking and talking (Hinsie & Campbell, pp. 445–446). A rapid shifting from one idea to the next is common, in which patients are highly distractable, changing from topic to topic in accordance with whatever stimuli strike them, Virginia Woolf, during her most serious attack, "entered into a state of garrulous mania, speaking ever more widely, incoherently and incessantly, until she lapsed into gibberish and sank into a coma" (Bell, Vol. 2, p. 25). At the height of these episodes she talked non-stop for four days and nights. Delusions of greatness frequently are manifested in mania. When Virginia was thirteen years old, on the verge of her first breakdown, she wrote an article describing a dream in which she was God. Intensified body sensations, common in mania, are exquisitely expressed in works such as *The Waves,* and often are related to the period of extreme infantile sensuality.

The manic polarity has been relatively neglected in the annals of psychiatric literature, as compared with the volumes published on depression. This phenomenon may be due to the difficulties of dealing with those troublemakers who cause great anxiety, demand much of the therapist's time, are socially disruptive, and perhaps more difficult to treat than any other diagnostic category. Research in recent years has been largely biochemical and genetic. Psychoanalytically, work on mania seems to have waned in the fifties. The little that was done deals mainly with fixations of psychosexual development. Freud himself deals with mania only in two short references (1917, p. 254 and 1921, p. 132), and mania is not even listed in the *Abstracts of the Standard Edition of the Complete Psycho-*

logical Works of Sigmund Freud (1973). His statement about mania, "Here are happenings rich in unsolved riddles," is almost as true today as it was then (Freud, 1933, p. 61).

In her landmark discussion of genius, Greenacre (1967, p. 57) remarks: "I am myself largely convinced that genius is a 'gift of the gods,' and is already laid down at birth, probably as a sport development (or mutation) which finds especially favorable soil for its evolution in families where there is also a good inheritance of intellect and a favorable background for identification."

If ever an artist met Greenacre's criterion for genius, that artist was Virginia Woolf. She was born on January 25, 1882, according to Bell (1972, Vol. 1, p. 18) because of "the imperfect art of contraception in the nineteenth century." There is no doubt that she began life as a sensitive, sensuous, superbly endowed individual. She belonged to one of England's great literary families. Her father was Sir Leslie Stephen, critic and editor of the renowned *Dictionary of National Biography*. His first wife was the daughter of Thackeray, and generations of his ancestors had been involved in literature. Virginia's great-grandfather, her grandfather, her uncle, and her cousin all were prominent authors. Her mother was Julia Jackson, herself a published writer, the granddaughter of a French nobleman who was page to Marie Antoinette. Virginia's sister Vanessa became a celebrated painter who married the critic Clive Bell, while her brother Adrian was a distinguished psychoanalyst, writer, and editor. Virginia herself married Leonard Woolf, author and publisher. Her closest friend and homosexual lover was Lady Vita Sackville-West, descendant of an ancient house of English nobility, and an illustrious poet and novelist of the times. Virginia's godfather was the great American poet, James Russell Lowell, one of a coterie of famous men and women who frequented the Stephen household, and to whom Virginia addressed her first recorded letter at the age of six. (See notes to Chapter 1, p. 178)

If Virginia Stephen at birth received the "gift of the gods," the devil apparently was represented as well. For it is widely accepted today in the psychiatric world that the disease of manic depression has an inherited, probably metabolic substructure (Jacobson, 1953, pp. 48–83; Fieve, 1975, pp. 1018–1022), and indeed, her biographer (Bell, 1972) reveals that many of her close relatives were known to be psychotic. Virginia's half sister Laura, a schizophrenic, was institutionalized most of her life. Sir Leslie Stephen, Virginia's father, had undergone a series of "nervous collapses" in his fifties. Virginia's cousin, the poet James Stephen, was a floridly psychotic manic-depressive, who took his own life at the age of thirty-three. Her uncle, the eminent James Fitzjames, deteriorated rapidly after the death of his son, became unable to function, and died two years later. Born to a family of geniuses and madmen, Virginia Stephen at birth was already a candidate for both of these human conditions.

SYMBIOSIS

To those basic ingredients of personality which combined to form her genius, Virginia's "choice" of mother added another dimension. Julia Stephen had a gift for symbiosis, the "stage of sociobiological interdependence between the 1-to 5-month-old infant and his mother" (Mahler, 1975, pp. 290–291). Mrs. Stephen and Virginia were wondrously matched the first four or five months of her life. Her writing makes clear that Mrs. Stephen was able to provide a luxurious sensual atmosphere which could lift the exquisitely endowed child to heights of ecstasy. Virginia later called these idyllic memories "the base upon which life stands." It was out of this base that the uniqueness of Virginia Woolf would emerge. In *Moments of Being* (1967, p. 66) Woolf describes one of her first memories, her early intoxication with her mother: "My mother would come out onto her balcony in a white dressing gown. There were passion flowers growing on the wall; they were great starry blossoms, with purple streaks, and large green buds . . . If I were a painter I should paint these first impressions in pale yellow, and silver, and green. Everything would be large and dim; and what was seen would be at the same time heard."

When the symbiotic period is joyful (as seems certain in the Mrs. Stephen–Virginia couple), the infant and mother have close body contact and bonding. This prepares the child of four or five months to follow normal developmental processes that lead away from mother. The good mother at this period of differentiation

"Great starry blossoms . . .

. . . with purple streaks"

"Passion flowers . . .

. . . growing on the walls." (Flower photography [pp. 26–27] courtesy
Margaret Ray.)

requires different psychological skills from those of the mother of infancy (Kaplan, 1978, p. 125). In contrast to the symbiotic mother, the mother of separation must be ready to allow the baby to explore, touch, and reach out to the world around him. Mrs. Stephen almost certainly was not as good a mother of separation as she was of symbiosis. According to Wolf and Wolf (1979, Part 1, p. 39), the character of Mrs. Ramsay in *To the Lighthouse* (1927), who Virginia states was modeled almost entirely upon that of her mother, sought continuous involvement with others to ward off a sense of inner emptiness and loneliness: "If one is a Mrs. Ramsay one can never let go of relationships because they all are needed to sustain life" (p. 41). Such a mother would find it impossible to allow her child to remain preoccupied or independent. Mrs. Ramsay muses on just such feelings (pp. 89–91): "Oh, but she never wanted James to grow a day older or Cam either. These two she would have liked to keep forever just as they were . . . nothing made up for the loss . . . Why should they grow up so fast? Why should they go to school? She would have liked always to have had a baby. She was happiest carrying one in her arms."

Masterson and Rinsley (1975, pp. 163–177) state that in the case of the future borderline or manifoldly unstable personality, the presence of pathology is a reflection not of a sudden or acute single trauma but rather of "a persistent, ongoing developmental failure, dating possibly from the mother's ambivalence toward the infant's earliest moves toward differentiation at about four or five months." I believe that the pathology of Virginia Woolf which led to her suicide also began at this early phase of development when the conflict between yielding to the magnetic pull of her mother and the strident organismic thrust toward development was unresolved.

Greenacre (1957, p. 55) in her discussion of the future genius states: "Rapid unfolding of the inner . . . pressure for unusual growth in some way [is] inherent in the child himself." Freud called such a state "a primal trend or urge that cannot be further resolved" (Hinsie & Campbell, 1977, p. 400). And such an intrapsychic conflict is intensified by the need to escape a clutching mother.

Woolf herself describes (1976, p. 79) the forces that wrenched her away from the engulfing grasp of her mother: "One must get the feeling that made her press on, the little creature driven on as she was by growth of her arms and legs, driven without her being able to stop it or to change it, driven as a plant is driven up out of the earth, up until the stalk grows, the leaf grows, buds swell."

Virginia differed from her less-endowed half sister, Stella, in the strength of her growth urge. The difference was a fateful one that, above all else, determined their divergent life paths.

STELLA

Virginia's fear of engulfment must have been reinforced by the tragic example of her half sister, Stella. Her stunted psychological development, as portrayed in *A Sketch of the Past* (1976, pp. 96–97), demonstrates the morbid consequences of yielding to Mrs. Stephen's magnetism. According to Kaplan (1978, p. 73), "Were the toddler to succumb to the absolute bliss of oneness before carving out his own space in the world, the child would be reabsorbed into the being of his mother. His surrender would be tantamount to ceasing to exist." Stella Duckworth, whom Virginia described as being "without any ambition or character of her own," yielded up her identity to be her mother's handmaiden. Her tragic life and early death must have served as further warning to Virginia that she must not yield to the allurement of her mother.

In *A Sketch of the Past* (1976, p. 96), one of her last works, Woolf reflects on the relationships between Stella and her mother after the death of Stella's father, Herbert Duckworth: "Stella as a child lived in the shade of . . . widowhood, saw that beautiful crape-filled figure daily; and perhaps took then the ply that was so marked—that attitude of devotion, almost canine in its touching adoration to her mother; that passive, suffering affection; and also that complete unquestioning dependence. . . . They were the sun and the moon to each other; my mother the positive and definite; Stella the reflecting and satellite. My mother was stern to her. All her devotion was given to George [the youngest son of Mrs. Stephen's first marriage], born posthumously and very delicate. . . . Stella she treated severely; so much so that before their marriage my father [Sir Leslie Stephen] ventured a protest. She replied that it might be true; she was hard on her daughter because she felt Stella 'part of myself.' A pale silent child I imagine her; sensitive; modest; uncomplaining, adoring her mother, thinking only how she could help her, and without any ambition or even character of her own.''

Although Stella had a governess to dilute the attachment to her mother, and developed certain skills, such as playing the violin, Virginia tells us (p. 97): "There was a stoppage in her [Stella's] mind, a gentle impassivity about books and learning . . . She thought herself so stupid as to be almost wanting.'' This kind of learning disability, "the stoppage of the mind,'' frequently is found, to a greater or lesser degree, in the development of symbiotic children whose egos have been subjected to their mothers' needs, necessitating the masochistic disowning of that part of themselves most threatening to the symbiotic parent (Roswell & Natchez, 1979, pp. 49–50).

"Stella was always the beautiful attendant handmaid, feeding her mother's vivid flame, rejoicing in the service, and making it the central duty of her life . . . She liked young men, she enjoyed their confidences, she was intensely amused by the play and intrigue of the thing; [only Stella, like so many symbiotic children] would insist upon going home, long before the night was over, for fear lest she be 'tired!' It was beautiful, it was almost excessive,'' Virginia continues insightfully, "for it had something of the morbid nature of an affection between two people too closely allied for the proper amount of reflection to take place between them; what her mother felt passed almost instantly through Stella's mind; there was no need for the brain to ponder and criticize what the soul knew . . . Stella was white as a ghost for days before she went abroad. . .''

That Stella survived only a few months after the death of her mother is history. That Virginia marked it so clearly reinforced the growth drive that propelled her *away* from her mother.

Unlike Stella, Virginia was unwilling to sacrifice her precarious selfhood in order "to live by that other clock that marks the approach of a particular person'' (1931, p. 273). She escaped that clock through the momentous push to action. As a result, she experienced a very different mother than the mother of symbiosis. Of this later mother, Woolf writes (1976, p. 83): "I can see now that she was living on such an extended surface that she had not

time, nor strength, to concentrate . . . upon me . . . Can I ever
remember being alone with her for more than a few minutes?''
According to Freud (1924, p. 149; 1924a, p. 183), the factor
that brings about psychosis is a conflict between the ego and a
reality that has become intolerable. On an ego level, Virginia Stephen chose to live by her own clock instead of her mother's. As
a result, she had to face the emotional withdrawal of her mother.
The actual death of Mrs. Stephen, which took place on the eve
of Virginia's adolescence (that period in which there is a second
biological upsurge toward individuation), was a repetition of her
great loss during the period of differentiation, a reality too terrible
to bear. Shortly after her mother died, Virginia experienced her
first psychotic breakdown.

Virginia clearly was able to ''carve out her own space in the
world.'' In her life, as well as in her work, she was able to establish
her uniqueness as a human being far more than was her half sister.
The following passage, however, indicates that in a psychological
sense she, like Stella, did not outgrow her symbiotic attachment
through a healthy process of individuation, but emotionally remained part of her mother forever. Standing by a flower bed at
St. Ives, Virginia muses (Woolf, 1976, p. 71): ''I was looking at
a plant with a spread of leaves, and it seemed suddenly plain that
the flower itself was part of the earth; that a ring enclosed what
was the flower, and that was the real flower; part earth, part flower.''

This theme, that each individual, incomplete unto himself, is
but part of a larger unit, appears and reappears throughout her
works. It climaxes in *The Waves* (1931), that unsurpassed study
of the establishment and dissolution of identity throughout the life
cycle. Thus it appears that all her life, Virginia Woolf was caught
in the conflict between losing herself in the pleasure of oneness
with mother and yielding to the clamorous organismic need to
develop.

HER "LOVE AFFAIR WITH THE WORLD"

According to Mahler (1965, Vol. 2, pp. 49–57), after the symbiotic period, the phase of differentiation from mother blends im-
perceptibly into the practicing period of separation individuation,

that time in a toddler's life (from fifteen to thirty-six months of age) when a massive shift of energy from the symbiotic partner to the autonomous apparatuses of the self and ego, such as walking, perception, and learning, takes place. After mastering most of the skills of relating his physical self to the outside world, he now devotes himself to practicing and refining his accomplishments. So absorbed is he by the excitement of exploring the new-found world that he forgets about his mother for long periods, and she no longer is the primary target for aggression or for love. Greenacre calls this period the "love affair with the world." Woolf called it the growth drive and the push to action.

While the practicing period is exhilarating for most toddlers, it must have been magnificent for Virginia, the artist. Imagine, for example, the exaltation experienced by the infant Virginia toddling down the hills of St. Ives to the "thick escallonia bushes whose leaves one picked and pressed and smelt" (p. 111); or see her energetically carrying oak apples and acorns back and forth among the great ferns of the Stephen children's "fairyland" playground (p. 115), or following with widening eyes the wonderful wandering butterflies soaring over the gardens (Bell, 1972). Her third memory, which took place during her second summer at St. Ives, hints of the love for her mother that became transformed into her love for the world: "All these colours and sound memories hang together at St. Ives," she wrote (1976, p. 66). "It still makes me feel warm; as if everything were ripe; humming; sunny; smelling so many smells at once . . . The gardens gave off a murmur of bees; the apples were red and gold; there were also pink flowers; and grey and silver leaves. The buzz, the croon, the smell, all seemed to press voluptuously against some membrane . . . It was rapture rather than ecstasy."

According to Freud (1917, p. 254), there must always be a shift in energy before the individual can experience exuberance. In all states, such as joy and triumph, a volume of previously inhibited energy suddenly becomes available. It seems reasonable to assume that the larger the volume of energy inhibited and suddenly released, the greater the degree of exaltation. For the biologically well-endowed infant Virginia, presumably constrained during the period of differentiation by a needy mother, the sudden release of power must have led to an ecstatic practicing period indeed. I believe it was this great upsurge of energy, originally suppressed by the wish to please her mother, that fueled the great organic forces released in Virginia's manic states.

The drive to action remained characteristic of Virginia all her life, even during many long periods between psychotic episodes. For example, her niece Angelica (Garnett, 1980) informs us: "Virginia danced around her [Vanessa] like the dragonfly round the water-lily, darting in to attack and soaring away before Vanessa could take action . . . Virginia's attitude was far from sitting, it was striding; long narrow thighs and shins in long tweed skirts, loping over the downs, across the water-meadows, beside the river, or thru the traffic in London, under the trees in the park and round the square. She was never placed, never quite at rest."

THE RAPPROCHEMENT CRISIS

We have left little Virginia Stephen at the height of her hard-won love affair with the world, entranced by the thrill of each new discovery, gleefully escaping engulfment by her mother. But alas, the enchantment of love rarely withstands the harsh light of reality! So it is for all children. And so it was for Virginia. About the middle of the second year, according to Mahler (1965, Vol. 2, pp. 49–57), the toddler abruptly "falls out of love." She who could conquer the world suddenly finds his omnipotence punctured. Her recently acquired skills and newly won territory suddenly seem less captivating. Life seems too hard to "go it alone." Dimly recalling the ease and bliss of earlier days, the prodigal toddler decides to "come home." What a shock to discover no one is there. Mother has made other plans. Virginia's place is now occupied by Adrian. There is no place for "baby" to return. Mahler terms this fateful crossroad the rapprochement crisis. Each child seals his or her future fate by the way he deals with this moment of truth. For Virginia, the crisis never was resolved, but was acted out all her life in alternating states of mania and depression, a dramatization of the rapprochement tragedy, the search for and loss of her mother.

What was the rapprochement crisis like for Virginia? Her biographies and works give a number of clues of her difficulties in dealing with this period. We know, for example (Woolf, 1976,

p. 114), that all her newfound skills could not get the moody cook Sophie to feed Virginia unless she felt like it. And perhaps of fateful importance, her sister Vanessa indicated that she and their brother Thoby had "some technique for making Virginia look purple with rage," and turn "the most lovely flaming red." Such experiences, in all likelihood, led to Virginia's feeling that she was "quite unable to deal with the pain of discovering that people hurt each other" (Woolf, 1976, pp. 71–72). Surely such feelings as these inspired Rhoda to say (*The Waves*, 1931, p. 224): "I shall fall alone through this thin sheet into gulf of fire. And thou will not help me. More cruel than the old torturers you will let me fall, and will tear me to pieces when I am fallen."

In a later work (1975, p. 48), Woolf says: "For the reason that it destroys the fullness of life, any break—like that of house-moving—causes me extreme distress; it breaks; it shallows; it turns the depth into hard thin splinters." It seems likely that the "first break that destroyed the fullness of life" occurred during the period when Virginia tried to reenter her mother's symbiotic orbit and found the position already occupied by her baby brother. Woolf's agony on the death of her mother (1976, p. 40) can best illuminate the effect on the twenty-two-month-old child of being displaced by Adrian: "It was the greatest disaster that could happen; it was as though on some brilliant day of spring the racing clouds of a sudden stood still, grew dark, and massed themselves; the wind flagged, and all creatures on earth moaned or wandered seeking aimlessly. . ."

Flush (1983), a story about Elizabeth Barrett Browning and her dog, delightfully unfolds a saga of dispossessed love in the setting of one of the most famous love stories in history. Flush, the most beloved of creatures, reigned on a purple pillow at the feet of his famous mistress until he was dethroned by his successor, Robert Browning. The painful rupture of his paradise, and the resulting agonies of jealousy he suffered sound autobiographical, and in all likelihood were inspired, originally at any rate, by Virginia's dethronement from her mother's lap.

An earlier reflection of Virginia's jealousy and vengefulness can be seen in the *Experiences of a Paterfamilias* (1892), her first recorded story written at the age of ten. It concerns the domestic foibles of a man and his wife, and centers on the husband's jealousy of the new baby. It begins (p. 5): "My wife a month ago got a child and I regret to say that I wish he had never been born, for I am made to give in to him on everything." The youthful Virginia found an interesting twist for her tale (p. 8). The new "father," she wrote, hung the baby on a tree, but it seems he stayed away "rather longer than I meant to be and when I came back I found the baby gone!"

A letter concerning her sister Vanessa's new baby, Julian, suggests that Virginia at age twenty-six had not changed her sentiments very much in regard to infants. Woolf writes (1975, p. 331): "I doubt that I shall ever have a baby. Its voice is too terrible, a senseless scream, like an ill-omened cat. Nobody could wish to comfort it, or pretend that it was a human being."

Interestingly enough, Virginia's much maligned baby brother grew up to become the eminent psychoanalyst and editor of the *International Journal of Psychoanalysis,* Dr. Adrian Stephen, who, in his article "On Defining Psychoanalysis" (1931), became an authority on sibling rivalry. Dr. Stephen's article, however, did not illuminate his sister's illness. It took later discoveries of Freud (1938, pp. 271–278) to point out that certain children, afraid of losing their mother's love, begin very early to split the good and bad mother images and to direct the anger against themselves. This mechanism preserves the image of a loving mother, but causes a feeling of helplessness in the child, which according to Bibring (1953) creates the basis for responding habitually with negative mood swings. Virginia Woolf in the following passage (1976, p. 71) bears out these theories: "I was fighting with Thoby on the lawn. We were pommeling each other with our fists. Just as I raised my fist to hit him, I felt: Why hit another person? I dropped my hand instantly, and stood there, and let him beat me. I remember the feeling. It was as if I became aware of something terrible; and of my own powerlessness. I shrink off, feeling horribly depressed." Here we can see clearly that Virginia at a very young age was unable to let herself experience anger at a loved one, and preferred to experience a depressed mood herself. This was an early manifestation of the psychological defense mechanism that eventually led to her death.

While Virginia clearly had difficulty accepting the birth of Adrian, we must ask *why* she was unable to take it in stride. According to Mahler (1966, pp. 152–168), a child who has problems accepting the birth of a sibling *already* has experienced difficulties during an earlier phase of development. According to Anna Freud (1948, pp. 41–42), it is love that tames aggression and renders it useful for the further development of the personality. Because of early difficulties with her mother, Virginia did not have available this refined form of aggression to help stabilize her personality. Also, raw or unneutralized rage becomes highly charged and difficult to control when it breaks into consciousness. It was this untamed anger that was released in Virginia's manic periods and powered the boundless energy that wreaked havoc during her high periods. Thus Virginia, because of her inability to cope with rage adequately, probably entered the age of rapprochement psychologically unprepared to master the problems of a new era.

THE RAPPROCHEMENT CROSSROADS

In the opinion of Mahler, Pine, and Bergman (1975, p. 107), the rapprochement period is a crossroads in which three great instinctual currents mingle and must be mastered: (1) the beginning of superego development, the aspect of the psyche that ensures ethical behavior, cultural standards, and self-criticism; (2) the contradictory urges of toilet training, in which the child is conflicted between conforming to the wishes of his parents and his own freedom to defecate at will; and (3), penis envy, the Freudian supposition that the little girl envies the male genitals and the power bestowed on the male by the possession of these organs. Let us speculate on the manner in which Virginia, already emotionally impaired, was able to deal with these crises.

1. Superego Development

In the formation of Virginia's superego, it seems that there were at least two areas in which her psychological development was immature. She had difficulty controlling her impulses, and was unable to regulate her own self-esteem. According to Meissner (1981, p. 47), when parental images have not been internalized, "the superego cannot assume the functions of parental control. Hence the individual remains dependent for these functions on the outside world." Virginia all her life was known for her inability to control her tongue, and much of Leonard's caretaking consisted of supervising Virginia's daily activities in order to maintain her emotional health. Virginia's "purple rages" inform us that her superego was not functioning well at the rapprochement crossroads. The following story (Bell, 1972, Vol. 1, p. 23), charming as it is, also predicts possible difficulties in the internalization of parental demands. The two-and-a-half-year-old Virginia had scratched her four-year-old brother and was told by her father to apologize. Virginia responded with "Why have we got nails, Papa?"

According to Jacobson (1957, p. 83), the constitution of the superego of the manic-depressive fails to have a modulating effect on the rises and falls of self-esteem and thus on mood control. Thus opinions of family and friends, as well as critics, greatly affected Virginia's moods, and statements such as "I rose in my own esteem because I rose in Mabel's" (1976, p. 187) bear out Jacobson's formulation. Bernard surely spoke for Virginia in *The Waves* (p. 116), when he said, "To be myself (I note) I need the illumination of other people's eyes, therefore cannot be entirely sure what is my self." In an attempt at self-healing, Virginia pursued the important women in her life with a vengeance. Bell (1972) states: "As a child she would ask her sister 'Do you like me better than. . .?' naming a list of friends and relatives. As a woman in her fifties she played the same game with Vanessa, who could never adequately respond to her sister's declarations of love . . . To satisfy that need, as imperative, in its way, as a junkie's, Virginia turned to women of a different sort, to women who had retained the knack of expressing simple affection. But even when she obtained the enormous infusions of affection and esteem that she required, the effects soon wore off, for she did not have that irrational, unshakable sense of her own worth which . . . is found in people who have been extravagantly wanted and loved as children. . ."

2. The Conflicts of Toilet Training

The investigation of that second great current of the rapprochement crossroads in Virginia, the conflictual urges of learning socially acceptable bathroom habits, present us with difficulties.

Since Woolf has recorded no memories of that aspect of her early life, and no other autobiographical material deals with it, either, we shall be forced to resort to what Freud (1937, pp. 257–269) called a "construction" or "reconstruction" in analysis in order to attempt to understand this important area of her development. The analyst's task, according to Freud, is "to make out what has been forgotton from the traces it has left behind, or, more correctly, to construct it." In other words, when a patient was unable to recollect the repressed memories which Freud considered the basis of that person's illness, Freud would encourage him to give himself up to free association in which Freud "could discover allusions to the repressed experiences and derivatives of the suppressed affective impulses as well as the reactions against them." When the patient was unable to recapture these repressed experiences, out of the bits and pieces of unconscious material revealed in his associations Freud would construct what he thought took place in the patient's history. When the analytic work is well done, Freud informs us that we produce in such a patient "an assured conviction of the truth of the construction which achieves the same therapeutic result as a recaptured memory." Nevertheless, Freud was careful to warn his readers that "We do not pretend that an individual construction is anything more than a conjecture which awaits examination, confirmation or rejection."

Since we do not have "the patient," Virginia Woolf, before us to confirm or deny our speculations, we, like the psychoanalyst, will attempt to use her writing and the anecdotes about her as free associations to help understand certain problems in her personality. These include the recurring depressions at the completion of each of her major works, her pathologically low feelings of self-worth, the need for constant affirmation, and why she could not bear to look upon any of her published works. We offer this construction with the hope that it will be useful in understanding Virginia Woolf's personality, and with the implicit understanding that, like Freud, we only intend our speculations as "a conjecture which awaits examination, confirmation or rejection."

Vanessa Bell (Bell, Vol. 1, pp. 28–29) relates an incident that illustrates how her mother received Virginia's later presentations, which perhaps can give us an idea of how her earliest productions were accepted. Virginia, age ten, was the chief writer of a little newspaper published by the Stephen children, called "The Hyde Park Gate News." Virginia and Vanessa surreptitiously laid a new copy of the paper on the table next to Mrs. Stephen. They then crept into the next room to watch their mother's reaction. Vanessa reported that Virginia "trembled with excitement." They could see their mother's figure outlined in the lamplight. For a long time, Mrs. Stephen ignored the paper. Then she picked it up and began to read. The girls held their breath. "Rather clever, I think," said Mrs. Stephen, and laid the paper down. Her response, according to Vanessa, "was enough to thrill Virginia." If she could be "thrilled" by such a comment, it would seem that her mother's praise must have been rare indeed. Mrs. Stephen's dying words to Virginia, "Hold yourself straight, my little Goat," suggest the usual tone of their interactions (1976, p. 84).

The newspaper incident, in capsule form, reveals Virginia's latent psychosis. Intimidated by a sense of worthlessness, Virginia needed her mother's approval in order to "measure her own stature." After receiving a positive response from Mrs. Stephen, Virginia, with great excitement, was able to overthrow her inner voices of self-criticism and doubt. In so doing, she behaved as a typical manic, who, after succeeding in getting rid of a crippling conscience, experiences a flood of excitation.

The analysis of numerous patients teaches us that when the infant's fecal offerings are devalued by the mother or the mother substitute, the child's self-esteem may be undermined for life. Material from her books leads me to believe that Virginia's "gifts," fecal and otherwise, met with little enthusiasm from Mrs. Stephen or her surrogate. An important passage from *Between the Acts* (1941, p. 209) suggests that Woolf, like her playwright, Miss LaTrobe, relied on affirmation from the outside world to counteract feelings that her gifts were worthless. At the successful conclusion of her play, Miss LaTrobe says: "The bells had stopped; the audience; also the actors; She could straighten her back. She could open her arms. She could say to the world, you have taken my gift! Glory possessed her—for one moment! But what had she given? A cloud that melted into the other clouds on the horizon. It was in the giving that the triumph failed. Her gift meant nothing. If they had understood her meaning . . . if the pearls had been real and the funds illimitable—it would have been a better gift. Now it had gone to join the others. A failure, she groaned, and stooped to put away the records."

The history of Virginia's early toilet training could easily be recorded in the above paragraph. Miss LaTrobe's pleasure in the giving of her gift may well parallel the infant Virginia's joy in presenting her mother or her nurse with her first fecal offerings. Like most individuals of that era, Mrs. Stephen probably did not understand her baby's strivings for mastery over the process of toilet training. In all probability, she did not realize that feces were her daughter's gift of love to her. Thus she would have been unable to instruct her staff to toilet-train her children gently. When the mother or nanny reacted with minimal interest or worse, the infant Virginia, in all likelihood, was crushed, her "triumph failed." "Her gift meant nothing." The "pearls were not real" to the mother (or her surrogate) as they were to the child. Her "funds were not illimitable." So Virginia, as many children, probably finished her first consciously directed bowel movement with a sense of failure and self-hatred that lasted all her life.

In adulthood, Woolf's triumph, like that of Miss LaTrobe's, was in her writing. At the conclusion of each of her major works, she experienced a terrifying depression. Many of her major novels ended with Woolf entering a psychotic episode. It is a matter of record that Virginia Woolf could not bear to reread anything she had written, and that any copy of a journal in which she had published was ruined for her forever. "Is the time coming," she wailed, "when I can endure to read my own writing in print without blushing—shivering, and wishing to take cover?" (1954, p. 11). It seems to me that Mrs. Stephen's rejection of Virginia's productions during the bathroom training period may well have been the paradigm of her later failure to meet her own standards. These painful feelings of inferiority characteristically were warded off by a return to the "love affair with the world," when she was the queen who could do no wrong. This regression was symptomatic of Virginia in mania, in creativity, and in a mood often characteristic of her even in well periods. But each "love affair," unfortunately, was punctured by life, just as her original image had been crushed by her mother, and Virginia relapsed each time into depression.

3. *Penis Envy*

The third great instinctual current to be mastered during the period of rapprochement is that of penis envy, or envy of the father's or brother's sexual differences and the power these differences gave them during the era in which they lived. Virginia Woolf was a feminist 50 years before feminism became popular. Pippett (1953, p. 12) suggests that "As a little girl Virginia would like to have been the one thing she could not be, a tom-boy." Despite the cultural and social climate of the times, in which men were the grossly favored sex, various passages in Woolf's work suggest that envy of males and feelings of castration played a central role in her pathology. Virginia's overwhelming feelings of jealousy may well have found their impetus at the birth of Adrian, her mother's favorite. For Bell (1972) states that "in the nursery it was believed that all Stephens were born with tails seven inches long."

In her famous treatise on feminism, *A Room of One's Own* (1929, pp. 10–18), Woolf wrote a hilarious comparison of food served to men and women scholars at the fictitious University of Oxbridge. In it she showed how the dinners symbolically illustrated the status of the sexes at the time. The men were served the "whitest of sauces, partridges many and varied, with all their retinue of sauces and salads—the sharp and the sweet; their sprouts foliated as rosebuds." The women were fed gravy soup, and plain beef with attendant greens and potatoes, "a homely trinity" suggesting to Woolf "the rumps of cattle in a muddy market." Associating this outrageous discrimination to the plight of the Manx cat, that "tailless creature from the Isle of Man," Woolf asks "Was he really born so, or had he lost his tail in an accident? The tailless cat . . . is rarer than one thinks. It is strange what a difference a tail makes. . ."

If the Oxbridge meals refer to the food of love served to Virginia and her brother Adrian in the nursery, and if the "cat without a tail," the castrated Virginia, gets to eat only "the rumps of cattle in a muddy market," no wonder Virginia refused to eat during her psychotic periods. For the feminist Virginia Woolf, who turned down medals and doctorates at universities which discriminated against women, second-class citizenship was unacceptable. And

if only a boy with a penis can "think well, love well, sleep well
. . . dine well," no wonder Virginia Woolf left behind her a history
of homosexuality, her continuing attempt to penetrate the mas-
culine paradise and reunite with her lost mother.

FURTHER HINTS OF TROUBLE

Mahler (1979, Vol. 1, p. 116) informs us that children who
have experienced earlier difficulties are "more readily depleted"
during the rapprochement phase. They get angrier than other children, which Bowlby (1960, pp. 9–52) called their "continued protest." These descriptions are characteristic of Virginia, who was
considered a child too fragile to attend school and remained shel-
tered and fatigued much of her life. Her "purple rages of a lovely
flaming red" and the atmosphere of "thunderous and oppressive
gloom" generated by her in the nursery suggest a "continued protest" of fury of a pathological nature.

Another indication of troubles to come is pointed out by
Mahler, Pine, and Bergman (1975, p. 107), who observe that the
ambivalence conflict in troubled children is expressed during the
period of rapprochement "in rapidly alternating clinging and neg-
ativistic behavior." Woolf beautifully describes this conflict in
her second novel, *Night and Day* (1920, p. 60): "It seems to . . .
[Mary] that Katherine possessed a curious power of drawing near
and receding, which sent alternate currents through her far more
quickly than was usual and kept her in a condition of curious
alertness." This "curious power" apparently invaded all of Virginia's relationships, for Bell (1972, Vol. 2, p. 59) states that
"There was no one whose stock did not rise and fall in the uncertain market of her regard."

BASIC MOODS

According to Mahler (1966, pp. 152–168), each subphase of
separation-individuation has a basic mood most characteristic of
it, which "leaves its mark upon the individual throughout the life
span." As a manic-depressive, Virginia Woolf alternated between
two basic moods all her life. The depressive mood, in all likelihood,

crystallized during the rapprochement period when Virginia first became aware that she and her mother were two separate people. At this time, in all likelihood, she felt as did Bernard in *The Waves* (1931, p. 67) when he said, "I do not believe in separation. We are not single. . ." This "dark part of the human condition" is superbly described by Rhoda in *The Waves* (1931, pp. 292–293). "Lord, how unutterably disgusting life is!. . . . Here we are among the bread crumbs, and the stained napkins again. That knife is already congealing with grease. . . . Always it begins again; always there is the enemy. . . . Call the waiter. Pay the bill . . . We must pull ourselves up out of our chairs. We must find our coats. We must go . . . Must, must, must—detestable word. Once more, I who had thought myself immune, who had said 'Now I am rid of all that,' find that the wave had tumbled me over, head over heels, scattering my possessions, leaving me to collect, to assemble, to heap together, summon my forces, rise and confront the enemy."

But Virginia Woolf's most characteristic mood was elation. In her well periods, she was filled with the delight of discovery experienced by the practicing infant. Bell (1972, Vol. 2, pp. 96–97) expertly captures this quality: "It was in movement that she was most truly herself. Then she reminded one of some fantastic bird, abruptly throwing up her head and crowing with delighted amusement at some idea, word, some paradox, that took her fancy. Her conversation was full of surprises, of unpredictable questions, of fantasy and of laughter—the happy laughter of a child who finds the world more strange, more absurd and more beautiful than anyone could have imagined."

BECK'S PORTRAIT

Beck (1967, pp. 90–94) paints a picture of the manic patient which in many ways resembles that of a practicing toddler. It parallels a brilliant portrait of Virginia Woolf. Excerpts of this description are as follows: "[The manic] . . . conveys a picture of complete lightness of heart . . . such as 'I am bursting with joy . . .' [is] capable of getting gratification from a wide variety of experiences and the intensity of his gratification far exceeds that of his normal phase . . . a leaf falling from a tree may cause feelings

of ecstasy . . . experiences a sense of a thrill when he thinks about
. . . or talks about himself and is very pleased and satisfied with
all his attributes . . . plunges into his various interests with abun-
dant zest. He experiences a broadening as well as an intensification
of interests . . . full of fun . . . optimistic about anything he un-
dertakes . . . tends to deny the possibility of any personal weakness, deficiencies, or problems . . . sheds the dependency that
was manifest. . . . In his expansive way he wishes to take in
everything life has to offer and at the same time demonstrate
to an increasingly greater extent his superior attributes . . . in
summary, he tends to be energetic, aggressive, animated, and
overactive; He presents a demeanor of impulsivity, boldness,
and lack of inhibition. He is generally sociable, genial, and exhibi-
tionistic.''

The similarity between the boundless energy of the manic
patient and that of the infant of the practicing period cannot be
a coincidence. Manics frequently are well-endowed individuals
who have experienced a particularly lavish practicing period. The
terror of engulfment experienced later in life by these people leads
to a grossly distorted reenactment of the practicing period. But
in the psychotic contortions of mania, the beautiful "love affair
with the world" becomes a caricature of its former state, making
grotesque what once was joyous. The manic condition is a desperate compromise between avoiding dissolution of self and the
warding off of painful reality. In order to escape unspeakable pain
and grief at terrible crises of her life, Virginia Woolf experienced
a tremendous pull back to her early paradise. She faced a double
jeopardy: Regression meant loss of self, while growing up meant
loss and dispair. To avoid these twin disasters, Virginia "chose"
the middle path of mania.

According to Eissler (1953, pp. 104–143), a defense mechanism may be used regressively or progressively. Some defenses,
like reaction formation, which turns an emotion into its opposite,
can shape anger into kindliness, and selfishness into saintliness,
to protect the ego. Others, like self-destructiveness, can demolish
it. In my opinion, Virginia Woolf, as all manics, distorted one of
nature's most beautiful and creative growth periods, that of the
"love affair with the world," into a hideous travesty. In her case,
the defense of mania met both extremes of Eissler's specification.

Regression to the practicing period of separation individuation helped to exalt her art to its loftiest peaks, and to steer her descent into madness and the depths of human despair.

SUMMARY

Virginia Stephen was a member of one of England's great literary families, many of whom were also mentally ill. An exquisitely endowed infant, she was beautifully matched with her mother during the early symbiotic period of development, the first few months of life. Woolf later called this period "the base upon which life stands."

Difficulties presumably began as early as the differentiation phase of development, when the infant, at about the age of four or five months, faintly begins to understand he is not his mother. Mrs. Stephen appeared to be a narcissistic woman, who required constant affirmation from those about her, and thus was unable to respond sufficiently to the requirements of a developing toddler.

Virginia, through her own inherent growth needs, probably was rescued from the fate of her half sister, Stella, whose psychological development was cannibalized by the needs of her mother. Unlike Stella, Virginia experienced a powerful biologically determined thrust toward separation-individuation between the ages of nine to fifteen months. This great organismic surge of energy in all likelihood is as characteristic of toddlers who are incipient manics as of children of future genius. Because of the magnetic attraction exerted by Mrs. Stephen, it is likely that Virginia experienced a particularly high-powered glee in evading the field of her mother. These high spirits, according to Freud, are characteristic of the manic as he overthrows the imprisoning restraints of his superego.

Deflated by events beyond her control, such as the sadistic treatment by her siblings, Virginia, like all children, attempted to return to her mother. But it appears that Mrs. Stephen was not available to her, in part because Virginia had been replaced by her new brother, Adrian. In an attempt to hold on to the love of her mother, Virginia split off her anger from consciousness and turned it against herself. As a result, this anger was not available for normal use in the building blocks of personality, such as the capacity to control impulses, internal regulation of self-esteem, and the ability to tolerate separation. These deficits were primary, leaving her vulnerable to depression and psychological collapse. The raw rage lay smoldering within until it finally burst forth to power her manic attacks.

The failure of rapprochement with her mother presumably already deflated Virginia in the nursery, and resulted in a basic mood of depression. She also experienced a second basic mood, elation, which was characteristic of her even in healthy periods and resembles the description of the typical manic victim given by Beck.

It is suggested that Virginia Woolf regressed to the practicing period of separation-individuation as a compromise formation to ward off the depressive mood on one hand, and regression to the period of symbiotic oneness and loss of self on the other. It is further suggested that regression to the practicing period as a defense mechanism is characteristic of the disease of manic depression.

2

Leslie Stephen
"That Ole Wretch, the Dearest of Creatures"

We have seen the enormous effect of Julia Stephen's narcissism on Virginia's personality formation. Let us now investigate the character of Virginia's father, Leslie Stephen, and the manner in which he influenced the development of her psychic structure. Perhaps this will help us understand his contribution to her psychosis, her genius, and eventual suicide. It also may cast some light on the comparative importance of heredity and environment in the genesis of Virginia Woolf.

THE TRIP TO THE LIGHTHOUSE

To begin with, let us examine the negative and positive effects of Leslie Stephen's character on Virginia as revealed in *To the Lighthouse* (Woolf, 1927). In this autobiographical novel (Woolf, 1954, pp. 76–77), the trip to the lighthouse symbolizes the many vagaries in the life of the Stephen family. The book, which is divided into three parts, can be analyzed into various time spans which represent the development of Virginia Stephen's life and character. The first section, entitled "The Window," illustrates the evolution of Virginia's personality during her early life with

Godevey's Lighthouse, Saint Ives

Cardis Bay, Saint Ives today

her mother. The period covered in this section, which ends with her mother's death, dramatizes part of the material discussed in Chapter 1 (see Bond, 1985). The second section of the novel, entitled "Time Passes," symbolizes the seven-year hiatus of Virginia's dissolution and despair following the death of Mrs. Stephen. It also represents the aftermath of Virginia's early failure to connect emotionally with her mother. The third section, "The Lighthouse," emphasized in this chapter, describes the reconstruction of the family and Virginia's personality around the persona of her father. It also symbolizes Virginia Stephen's failure to resolve her Oedipus complex. (See notes to Chapter 2, p, 182)

Leslie Steven is introduced in the book as Mr. Ramsay, a man who behaves sadistically, delighting in "the pleasure of disillusioning his son and casting ridicule upon his wife." This set off feelings of murderous rage in his children (ibid., p. 10). For example, when the family joyfully anticipated a boat trip to the lighthouse, Mr. Ramsay was pleased to inform them that the weather was sure to be bad. "Had there been an axe handy, or a poker, any weapon that would have gashed a hole in his father's breast and killed him, James [Virginia's brother, Adrian] would have seized it. Such were the extremes of emotion Mr. Ramsay excited in his children's breasts. . ." To make matters worse, Mrs. Ramsay, like many women of her time, was a poor role model in this respect, submitting regularly to her husband's tyranny with feeble responses, such as, "But it may be fine—I expect it will be fine."

Mr. Ramsay prided himself on his honesty and realism (Stephen, 1977, p. 10). According to him, "He was incapable of untruth; never tampered with a fact; never altered a disagreeable word to suit the pleasure or convenience of any mortal being." Nevertheless, in *To the Lighthouse,* Woolf presents him quite differently. In sharp contrast to his own inflated image, she portrays her father as an emotionally dishonest creature who blusters, bullies, and manipulates. That this behavior was as characteristic of Leslie Stephen as it was of Mr. Ramsay is borne out by Stephen's own observations about his treatment of his sister-in-law, Anni (ibid., p. 23): "I had a perhaps rather pedantic mania for correcting her flights of imagination and checking her exuberant impulses," he wrote. "Anni and Minnie [his first wife] used to call me the cold bath for my habit of drenching Anni's little schemes and fancies with chilling criticism.'' To his children, who both idealized and hated him, the discrepancy between Stephen's words and actions must have led to denial, confusion, and distortion of reality.

Woolf considered Stephen's treatment of his family the worst of possible fates, as indicated by the ruminations of Virginia's childhood counterpart "Cam," in *To the Lighthouse,* who states (p. 222): "It struck her, this was tragedy—not palls, dust, and the shroud; but children coerced, their spirits subdued."

The scene describing the anticipation of the boat trip is also interesting in the anamnesis of Virginia's illness. The father's hostile pessimism punctures the joyous mood of the family. In rapid succession the children experience rapture and despair, suggesting that Virginia's manic depression could have been accentuated by the contrasting temperaments of her parents. It is conceivable that a child could accept the vagaries of an unduly optimistic parent or a deflating pessimistic one. But these rapidly shifting ego states are so dissonant that they seem difficult if not impossible to integrate.

Kushen states (1981, p. 284): "The problem of integrating her self-images, the way she saw herself at different times and ages in different situations, the problem of synthesizing various physical and characterological traits, was a chronic and at times devastating one for Virginia Woolf." In *Orlando* (1928, pp. 308–309) Woolf speaks of her many selves: "These selves of which we are built up one on top of another, as plates are piled on a waiter's hand, have attachments elsewhere, sympathies, little constitutions and rights of their own, call them what you will (and for many of these things there are no name) so that one will only come if it is raining, another in a room with green curtains, another when Mrs. Jones is not there, another if you can promise a glass of wine—and so on; for everybody can multiply from his own experience the difficult terms which his different selves have made with him—and some are too wildly ridiculous to be mentioned in print at all."

Love (1977, p. 49) quotes Bell to the effect that "the differences between her maternal and paternal relatives led Virginia to say that two very contradictory bloodstreams clashed in her veins, creating conflicts and polarities in her." Love then concludes,

"Certainly two very different traditions met and, in some manner, clashed in her parents' marriage." Woolf valiantly sought to master the difficulties caused by her parents' discrepancies through use of her creative abilities (Hartmann, Kris, & Loewenstein, 1949). For example, in many of her novels, notably *Night and Day* (1919) and *To the Lighthouse,* she developed the theme of contradictory views of the world, and the internal and interpersonal conflicts they caused her. Yet, as always when basic issues are unresolved, her creative efforts to integrate them were only temporarily successful.

Woolf makes it clear that those close to her father had to shut their eyes to his shortcomings. They had to flatter and admire him, while ignoring his self-deceptions. Such children often have to distort reality in order to maintain the idealized image required by the parent for psychological survival (Laing, 1964). Leslie Stephen exacted just such a sacrifice on the part of his family. Such distortion made a significant contribution to Virginia's pathology.

Obviously, Leslie Stephen was a complex man. Despite the exigencies of living with him, he was a brilliant, productive person with many endearing qualities. The appalling contradictions in his character led Virginia to call him "That ole wretch, the dearest of creatures" (Love, 1977, p. 14). Lily Briscoe, who represents the artistic aspects of Woolf's nature in *To the Lighthouse* (1927, p. 40) describes Stephen's counterpart, Ramsay, as "petty, selfish, vain, egotistical, he is spoilt; he is a tyrant; he wears Mrs. Ramsay to death; but he has . . . a fiery unworldliness; he knows nothing about trifles; he loves dogs and his children." It is evident from Woolf's writing that she felt her father loved his children, and in his own way he loved his wife. Stephen himself says (*The Mausoleum Book,* p. x): ". . . whatever faults I had and however many troubles I incidentally caused, I loved her from first to last with my whole soul and . . . she knew it." But the conflicting emotions aroused by these contradictory qualities made life with him even more exasperating.

Lily Briscoe illustrates this trait of Mr. Stephen's in her description of his counterpart, Mr. Ramsay, in *To the Lighthouse* (pp. 221–223) and his effect on her. After Mrs. Ramsay's death, Lily concerns herself with a painting problem that has preoccupied her throughout the book. Just as she is about to resolve it, Mr.

Ramsay comes bearing down upon her. Lily became paralyzed. "She could not paint. She stooped, she turned; she took up this rag; she squeezed that tube. But all she did was to ward him off a moment. He made it impossible for her to do anything . . . she could only think, But he'll be down on me in a moment, demanding . . . That man, she thought, her anger rising in her, never gave; that man took. She, on the other hand, would be forced to give. Mrs. Ramsay had given. Giving, giving, giving, she had died. . ."

Leslie Stephen's contradictory character is borne out further by Woolf's journal on her father's birthday in 1928 (*A Writer's Diary*, p. 138). "He would have been 96, 96 yes, today; but mercifully was not. His life would have ended mine. What would have happened? No writing, no books;—inconceivable." This very conflict, between the wish to yield and the need to maintain her selfhood, is a repetition of the great struggle Virginia experienced during the rapprochement phase of separation individuation. Virginia Woolf, then, was relieved by the death of her father, for so long as he lived, he left her no room to exist.

In *To the Lighthouse*, James (her brother, Adrian) also has much to say about his father's merciless domination (pp. 273–274). When the family finally goes to the lighthouse under the leadership of his father, Mr. Ramsay sits reading while James sails the boat. "James felt that each page was turned with a peculiar gesture aimed at him . . . and all the time, as his father . . . turned one after another of those little pages, James kept dreading the moment when he would look up and speak sharply to him about something or other. . . . Why were they lagging about here? he would demand, or something quite unreasonable like that . . . James thought, I shall take a knife and strike him to the heart . . . Whatever [James] did—whether he was in a business, in a bank, a barrister, a man at the head of some enterprise, [he vowed that] he would fight, track down and stamp out—tyranny, despotism, he called it—making people do what they did not want to do, cutting off their right to speak." "James" kept his word. For he grew up to become Dr. Adrian Stephen, the noted psychoanalyst who devoted his days to helping people discover their "right to speak."

Virginia, too, became the voice of freedom, suggesting that James's wish belonged to her as well as her brother. She fought for rights for women. As one of the earliest feminists, she raised her voice against male tyranny, notably in *A Room of One's Own* (1929) and *Three Guineas* (1938), and demanded "the right to speak" for suppressed women everywhere. But instead of "taking a knife and sticking [her] father to the heart," she struck again and again with her pen.

It would be difficult for a daughter under any circumstances to resist her father's magnetism. For a child who loved him as intensely as Virginia, it was almost impossible. What Virginia felt at those moments is suggested by Lily's ordeal in *To the Lighthouse* (p. 226): "All Lily wished was that this enormous flood of grief, this insatiable hunger for sympathy, this demand that she should surrender herself up to him entirely . . . should leave her, should be diverted . . . before it swept her down in its flow . . ." But Virginia's urge to yield to her father coexisted along with enormous rage and frustration, with "passionate affection . . . alternating with passionate hatred of him."

It seems to me that the child Virginia took the only path possible to master the overwhelming quantity of conflicting excitations. She identified with her father, and behaved in much the same manner as Stephen did with his family. As a result, her nephew, Quentin Bell (1972, Vol. 2, p. 59), was able to state that "There is no one who doesn't go up and down in the stock market of her regard." Virginia's clashing messages left people in much the same confusion she felt with her own father.

The Parental Relationship

The way Virginia viewed her parents' relationship was important to the development of her identification with them. A revealing description of their behavior is given by Lily Briscoe (*To the Lighthouse*, pp. 295–297) as she daydreams of the gentlemanly manner in which Ramsay treated his wife during their courtship. We can surmise from Lily's fantasy that the Stephens at least sometimes had a loving sexual relationship, and that Stephen often treated his wife with respect and devotion. The sexuality in the Ramsay marriage is suggested symbolically (p. 107) when the couple walk off arm in arm after an argument. Mrs. Ramsay experiences a thrill of sexual pleasure as she notes the shape and firmness of her husband's arm, even though he is over sixty. Clearly Virginia noted her parents' romance and was envious, and at one time had reached the oedipal level where she was able to maintain her love for her father despite her fear of him. But it is evident from Woolf's life history that subsequent developments forced her to abandon the optimal oedipal solution, that of identifying with her mother and finding an adequate substitute for her father.

Virginia's alter ego, Lily, casts light on these developments (*To the Lighthouse*, p. 296): "But it would be a mistake, she thought, thinking how they walked off together, arm in arm, past the greenhouse, to simplify their relationship . . . it was no monotony of bliss—she with her impulses and quicknesses; he with his shudders and groans. Oh, no. The bedroom door would slam violently early in the morning. He would start from the table in a temper. He would whizz his plate through the window. Then all through the house there would be a sense. of doors slamming and blinds fluttering . . . But it tired Mrs. R., it cowed her a little— the plates whizzing and the doors slamming. And there would fall between them sometimes long rigid silences . . . After a time he would hang back stealthily about the places where she was— roaming under the window where she sat writing letters or talking, for she would take care to be busy when he passed . . . and pretend not to see him. Then he would turn smooth as silk, affable, urbane, and try to win her so . . . At length . . . he would say her name, and this time something in the tone would rouse her, and she would go to him . . . and they would walk off together among the pear trees, the cabbages, and the raspberry beds. They would have it out together . . . until it was time for dinner, and there they were, he at one end of the table, she at the other, as usual."

The Stephen marital relationship is also summed up by Rose (1978, pp. 158–159), who states that Woolf's portrait of her father as the self-torturing, self-pitying tyrannical killjoy of *To the Lighthouse* is substantiated by the record of his private life in *The Mausoleum Book* (Stephen, 1977), which records evidence of his "exasperating domestic tyrannies." For despite his worship of Julia, "he treated her somewhat as a servant, someone who should be constantly available, constantly supportive, constantly working to order his life. Hard on all the women who cared for him, he combined a theoretical veneration of women with actual condescension and harassment, demanding a total dedication to his own needs."

Mrs. Ramsay contributed to her husband's abusiveness by subjugating her own perceptions to his. If he said it would rain, she agreed. If he said it would not rain, she agreed to that, too (p. 51). It is not difficult to imagine the effect of her behavior on Virginia's ability to test reality, or to be self-assertive when she was in love.

Mr. Ramsay's weak self-esteem demanded idealization from others. To give him what he required to survive, Mrs. Ramsay had to deny her fury and turn it into reverence. But both paid dearly for their hypocrisy. Neither the participants nor the marriage matured. For example, Mrs. Ramsay retaliated by refusing to tell her husband she loved him. In *The Mausoleum Book*, Stephen feebly protested his wife's withholding and then quickly denied that he cared. It didn't really bother him, he protested, as her love was evident in her actions. But if Stephen deceived himself, he certainly didn't fool his daughter Virginia, who immortalized in *To the Lighthouse* the pain caused Stephen by his wife's revenge. Julia Stephen may even have paid for her duplicity with her life. According to Woolf (1976, p. 114), her mother "died of overwork easily at 49. He found it difficult to die of cancer at 72."

Imagine for a moment a young child "in love" with her father in the oedipal stage of development. Recapture for a moment this child's earliest years characterized by a terror of reengulfment into the undifferentiated stage of life. Then picture a father requiring his wife to give up needs of her own in order to meet his narcissistic claims. Then consider the kind of model this woman would make for a little girl already terrified at the thought of loss of self. In the normal flow of events, a little girl yearns to identify with her mother in order to master the problems of the oedipal period. But the little girl Virginia could not take the usual path to resolve her oedipal strivings. She could not model herself after Julia Stephen because her mother was the prime example of the child's worst nightmares come true. For Mother had lost her identity, and later, even her life.

This loss of self is poignantly depicted by Mrs. Ramsay (*To the Lighthouse*, pp. 95–96), in her description of how it felt after

her children went to bed. "For now she need not think about anybody. She could be by herself, by herself. And that was what now
she often felt the need of—to think; well, not even to think. To
be silent; to be alone." And by the lament of Julia Stephen, herself (Woolf, 1976, p. 92), "O the torture of never being left alone!"

So here is the child Virginia who cannot make use of whatever
possibilities the oedipal phase offers for mastering early conflicts.
At one point in *To the Lighthouse,* the children realize that through
the leadership of their father they eventually will reach their goal.
Virginia's childhood counterpart, Cam, says to herself (p. 304),
"This is right, this is it . . . Now I can go on thinking whatever
I like, and I shan't fall over a precipice or be drowned, for there
he is, keeping his eye on me." For Virginia Woolf, the writer,
her father's intellectual guidance and support indeed made it possible for her to "see the light" and attain her professional goals.
But it was not to be so on a permanent basis for Virginia Woolf,
the woman. Her emotional difficulties were compounded rather
than relieved at the oedipal stage of development. For identification with a mother who surrendered her selfhood had to be
avoided at all costs.

THE STRUGGLE TO DISENGAGE FROM MOTHER

In *Professions for Women* (1966, p. 284) Woolf describes how
the clash between parental identifications threatens to destroy her
writing career at its very onset, while she was trying to write her
first article, a review of a novel by a famous man. Woolf states
(p. 285):

"And while I was writing this review, I discovered that if I
were going to review books I should need to do battle with a
certain phantom. And the phantom was a woman, and when I
came to know her better I called her . . . The Angel in the House.
It was she who used to come between me and my paper when I
was writing reviews. It was she who bothered me and wasted my
time and so tormented me that at last I killed her . . . I will describe
her as shortly as I can. She was intensely sympathetic. She was
immensely charming. She was utterly unselfish. She excelled in
the difficult arts of family life. She sacrificed herself daily. If there

was chicken, she took the leg; if there was a draught she sat in it—in short she was so constituted that she never had a mind or a wish of her own . . . And when I came to write . . . [about] that novel by a famous man, she slipped behind me and whispered: 'My dear, you are a young woman. You are writing about a book that has been written by a man. Be sympathetic; be tender; flatter; deceive; use all the arts and wiles of our sex. Never let anyone know you have a mind of your own' . . . Had I not killed her she would have killed me. She would have plucked the heart out of my writing. For . . . you cannot review even a novel without having a mind of your own, without expressing what you think to be the truth about human relations, morality, sex. And all these questions, according to the Angel of the House, cannot be dealt with freely and openly by women. . ."

Although the above passage ostensibly describes Woolf's professional struggle against identification with her mother, the feeling expressed clearly is a derivative of her early struggle for sexual identity as well. That she never achieved an integrated sexuality in her writing or in her personal life is amply demonstrated in the essay and in the history of her bisexuality. The struggle in both arenas is dealt with in the following passages:

Woolf (1966) pictures herself lost in the creative process, immersed "as a fisherman lying sunk in dreams on the verge of a deep lake with a rod held out over the water." (The rod held over the lake in Freudian terms symbolizes her identification with father about to have intercourse with mother). "Suddenly," Woolf continues, "there was a smash, an explosion, foam, and confusion, which interrupted the creative process." Obviously, Virginia's sexual fantasies (including the homosexual aspects) had come too close to consciousness, and precipitated the anxiety that arrested her spurt of creativity. "The line raced through the girl's fingers," Woolf continued. "[She] was roused from her dream . . . Men, her reason told her, would be shocked . . . She could write no more. . . ." Woolf then continues with what for her was a very rare admission, that she was unable to deal with and understand her own female sexuality in her work. She states that she has never really solved the problem of "telling the truth about my own experiences as a body," and adds that "I doubt that any woman has solved it yet."

In the above episode, the girl "fisherman" is awakened by her fear that "men would be shocked" at her "passions unfitting for a woman." Women of the early twentieth century were taught that "good" women do not enjoy sex, and to submit to the animal natures of their husbands out of a sense of duty. In Woolf's case, this teaching must have been intensified, as her father (like all Fellows of Oxford and Cambridge) was an Anglican minister, who clearly made it known that he considered sex "a topic unsuited for discussion in literature" (Love, ibid., p. 43). Nevertheless, it seems to me that the overall character of her father was more pathogenic to the sexuality of the growing girl than the repressive mores of the times. For most women, including her mother, had sexual relations with their husbands. After a few abortive efforts early in her marriage, Virginia Woolf did not. And many women of the day, unlike Virginia, who "hated the physicalness of having children of one's own" (Woolf, 1954, p. 119), managed to have babies.

In this post-Freudian age, it is clear from other character traits that Virginia Woolf suffered grave psychological problems in feminine identity. For example, she was known to dress in a peculiar manner. People on the street often found her strange-looking, and on occasion were known to point to her odd gauzy layers fastened with safety pins, and to laugh. According to Rose (ibid., p. 7), "everything to do with dressing her body [was] painful and sometimes terrifying. She hated shopping, being fitted for clothes, wearing a new outfit. She could hardly bear to be photographed. Although she enjoyed nature outside of herself, anything connected with her body carried a burden of shame." This observation is particularly interesting when compared with her father's description of his style of dressing (1977, p. 35) that his college peers thought him "scandalously slovenly in dress and altogether wanting in the true social polish." Virginia's earliest memories of her mother's dresses are replete with sensual ecstasy. Nevertheless, it is her father's style of dressing with which she identifies, further suggesting the turmoil she must have suffered at the wish to be like her mother.

Be that as it may, Woolf preferred to explain her sexual "difficulties" sociologically rather than psychodynamically, as obstacles that were there for women rather than for men. Clearly, the pressures of society contributed significantly to the sexual and aggressive inhibitions that plagued early twentieth-century women. But after psychological damage has been stamped into one's character by society, it is necessary for the individual to look inward in order to produce internal change. This Virginia Woolf was unable or unwilling to do. As a result, Woolf's explanation of her sexual inhibitions is relatively superficial. It is likely that she remained asexual in her marriage less because she feared the wrath of her father ("Men would be shocked. . .") and therefore her own superego, than because she was terrified at the idea of loss of self in sexuality. This is borne out by the youthful Virginia's question to her friend, Violet Dickenson (1975, p. 505), after accepting Leonard's proposal of marriage. "But won't it be awful," she wrote, "if . . . my character, which promised so well, finally rots in marriage?" Clearly what Virginia experienced here was an oedipal updating of the old bugaboo that had plagued her from her earliest years, the fear of the pull to symbiosis.

In *Mrs. Dalloway* (Woolf, 1925, p. 10) Clarissa refuses to marry Peter Walsh, the man with whom she is in love. Rather, she marries for the external trappings of life, such as her social life. Peter would have tried to bring to life her central wooden core; but Clarissa had to reject the possibility of intense passion in her life in order to maintain "the privacy of her soul." Peter states that in refusing to marry him, she proved her frigidity. According to Rose (1978, p. 144), "One of Woolf's concerns in this novel is the strategic value of frigidity, its use in preserving a woman's sense of autonomy and selfhood." Rose is correct when she considers that Woolf's frigidity was in the service of self-preservation. But Rose fails to understand that the psychogenesis of terror of losing oneself long precedes the subjugation of the female in marriage.

IDENTIFICATION WITH FATHER

I have hypothesized that as a child Virginia Stephen had reached but not maintained the oedipal level of development. A story told by her sister Vanessa (V. Bell, 1956, pp. 3–4) about Virginia near the age of four strongly suggests that this hypothesis is correct. Vanessa says: "I remember one evening as we were jumping about naked, she and I, in the bathroom. She suddenly asked me which I liked best, my father or mother. Such a question seems to me rather terrible—surely one ought not to ask it. . . . However, being asked, one had to reply and I found I had little doubt as to my answer. 'Mother', I said, and she went on to explain why she, on the whole, preferred father . . ." Virginia's expressed preference for her father at age four is particularly interesting in the light of her statement (1939, p. 64)) when she was fifty-seven years old, that her love for her mother was "the base upon which life stands." It suggests that Virginia Woolf, at age fifty-seven, had not been able to maintain the lofty oedipal heights she had reached at the age of four.

So here we have little Virginia Stephen, age perhaps five, who loves her father dearly but is too terrified of her fantasies of wanting "to marry" him to allow them to surface very far. Her dilemma must have been great indeed. To regress in time was inordinately unsatisfactory; regression to the rapprochement stage brought on a nightmare of depression, regression to the practicing period resulted in a distorted manic "love affair with the world," while deeper regression to the symbiotic phase led to dissolution of self. Yet progression in an age-appropriate manner was unthinkable, for there were father's rages and puritanical views on sex, which made such wishes intolerable. Even more important were father's demands from his women for total negation of self. There remained for Virginia one escape; she could identify with her father. Then she could be at one with him forever, and symbolically possess her mother as well. I believe that this was the path taken by Virginia Woolf, the path that led *To the Lighthouse* of her genius, as well as to her homosexuality.

If one goes through the literature, it soon becomes apparent that Virginia resembled her father uncannily in character traits, in her writing and self-doubts, in her great and malicious sense of humor, in her marriage, in her frugality, in her fear of aging, and in her social consciousness. In many other attributes of her personality, it is evident that Leslie Stephen was her primary model. According to Annan (1984, pp. 134–135): "Virginia was in a real sense . . . flesh of his flesh and bone of his bone. She and her father were both tall and gaunt, great walkers. . . . like him she could turn a judicious, readable review; . . . like her he responded to poetry in words and rhythms. Both were charmers when they chose to be. Both burnt with rages . . . Money threw both into a panic. Neither ever stopped working . . . Both were put on the rack by unsympathetic reviews of their work. They both leant on women to give them support . . . For both, rejection and disappointment made existence insupportable." Stephen seemed pleased by this identification. When his daughter was only eleven years old, he wrote his wife (1977, p. xxviii): "Yesterday I discussed George II with Ginia . . . She takes in a great deal and will really be an author in time. . ." Virginia bore out her father's feeling many years later, when she wrote to Vita Sackville-West, "I was more like him than her I think: and therefore more critical; but he was an adorable man, and somehow, tremendous."

A vital aspect of Stephen's encouragement of Virginia's identification, for which posterity owes him a debt, occurred when he took over her intellectual development. In an important sense, Stephen became his daughter's mentor, and trained her to become his intellectual heir. Woolf (1976, p. 136) described her father's beautiful teaching methods, as she went into his study to get a new book. "There I would find him, swinging in his rocking chair, pipe in mouth. Slowly he would realize my presence. Then rising, he would go to the shelves, put the book back and very kindly ask me what had I made of it? Perhaps I was reading Johnson. For some time we would talk and then, feeling soothed, stimulated, full of love for this unworldly, very distinguished, lonely man, I would go down to the drawing room again. . ." Stephen himself was famous in his own century as an editor and author of note. He wrote and published at least 21 books in his lifetime, and was the founder and editor of the prestigious *Dictionary of National Biography*. By fostering the identification as writer and critic, as well as by serving as mentor and teacher, Leslie Stephen played a seminal role in the development and shaping of Woolf's literary genius.

Virginia Woolf, like her father, was known for speaking her mind. Unpleasant comments, fear of hurting another, or even reality itself did not stay her tongue. According to her brother-in-law Clive (Bell, Vol. 1, p. 124), nobody was less trustworthy than Virginia, the "perfect model of indiscretion." Perhaps Clive was wrong; Leslie Stephen was an even more perfect model. He taught his daughter that cruelty and self-indulgence at the expense of another is personally and socially acceptable.

Their office boy (Kennedy, 1972, pp. 18–19) has further comments: "She started talking about the Hogarth Press in a way that I thought didn't please Leonard very much, saying it was like keeping a grocer's shop. I think she is rather cruel in spite of the kind rather dreamy way she looks at you. She described Mrs. Cartwright as having the step of an elephant and the ferocity of a tiger . . . I consider it bad form to laugh at your employees."

According to Bell (1972, Vol. 1, p. 148), "Virginia's imagination was all accelerator and no brakes; it flew rapidly ahead, parting company with reality, and when reality happened to be a human being, the result could be appalling." The difficulty, in my opinion, was less Virginia's imagination than her inability to control it. Healthy people allow their impulses to remain in fantasy when it is wise to do so. Virginia could not. The problem, already apparent in the nursery, was exacerbated by Stephen's example of saying and doing whatever he felt like. He too was "all accelerator and no brakes." This defect in Virginia probably could have been remedied by a mature example on the part of her father. According to Herzog (1982), "The father's role was primarily that of the modulation of the aggressive drive and fantasy." But what is unthinkable behavior in most families was considered normal by Leslie Stephen. And his daughter followed in his calamitous footsteps.

Another aspect of her father's character adopted by Virginia was his rapid fluctuation of mood. According to Virginia herself (Bell, Vol. 1, p. 185), ". . . I am fearfully unstable. I pass from hot to cold in an instant, without any reason . . ." In *Leslie Stephen* (1969, p. 73), Woolf illustrates how her father could instantly change his manner, when it so suited him.

"Yet the unreasonable mood was superficial, as the rapidity with which it vanished would prove. The cheque-book was shut; pictures of ruined old age . . . and the workhouse were forgotten . . . Taking his hat and his stick, calling for his dog and his daughter he would stride off into Kensington Gardens. . ."

SUICIDE AS A MEANS OF AVOIDING IDENTIFICATION WITH HER AGING FATHER

As we have seen, Virginia Woolf's identification with her father was, by and large, the blueprint for her way of life. I believe it was instrumental in her choice of death as well, and that her suicide at age fifty-nine and a half was already predictable at the age of twenty-one, at the time of her father's terminal illness. "I begin to wish for anything to end this," she wrote then (1975, p. 125). "The waiting is intolerable . . . The worst of it is he is so tired and worn out, and wants to die . . . I shall do my best to ruin my constitution before I get to his age, so as to die quicker!" In her death letter to Leonard, Virginia wrote: "I cannot bear the thought of another bout of madness." What was unwritten, perhaps, was also the thought, "I cannot bear to become the wretch my father became when he reached my stage of life."

Leslie Stephen was fifty years old by the time Virginia was born. Woolf states (1969, p. 69) that by the time his children were growing up, the great days of her father's life were over. He had been a great walker and climber and he could not accept the waning of these skills with grace. Even more important was his feeling that he had failed as a writer (p. 75). In *To the Lighthouse*, we are told that Ramsay's last book was not up to the standards of his previous works, that ". . . what came after was more or less amplification, repetition." Virginia Woolf was always petrified on the publication of each of her works. Her standards were so high that her works were rarely seen by her as satisfactory. As noted earlier, she lamented, "A magazine in which a work of mine is published is ruined for me forever." Compare this with Leslie Stephen's critique of his own writing (1977, p. 94): "I am so touchy that I have long ceased to read reviews of myself; even praise often worries me."

According to Rose (1978, p. 161), "To succeed as a writer, Woolf found it necessary to model herself largely on her father." In so doing, she must have been terrified by the rapid approach of her seventh decade. She, like Stephen, had had great difficulties with her writing toward the end. Leonard, for the first time, had disliked one of her novels, *The Years* (1937), and had criticized the biography of *Roger Fry* (1940). Woolf herself rated her last book, *Between the Acts* (1941), as "completely worthless" (1980, pp. 485–6). "I have lost the art," she moaned, seven days before she took her life (1980, p. 456). Convinced that the quality of her work could only have deteriorated further, her suicide on the eve of that dreaded birthday may well have served to head off such a disaster.

THE TRANSMUTATION OF GRIEF INTO ART

Perhaps the most important means of identifying with her father was Virginia's ability to emulate his creative manner of transforming grief into art. For example, when his close friend Henry Fawcett died, Stephen set about writing his friend's biography for the *Dictionary of National Biography*. He did the same a few years later for his brother Fitzjames. But most important of all, little more than a fortnight after his wife Julia died, Leslie Stephen sought to assuage his terrible grief by beginning the *Mausoleum Book* (1977), the intimate story of his marriage. The therapeutic effects of the work are best demonstrated in a letter to his friend, Charles Norton (p. ix), written seven weeks after the death of Julia. In it, Stephen states:

"I am well in bodily health—only with a sense of utter exhaustion and want of interest in every outside thing . . . But—I will say one thing. I have passed these fearful weeks partly in putting together old letters and in writing a little document for the exclusive benefit of her children. I could do nothing else; but it has interested me and made me feel nearer to her. . ."

The letter makes clear that Stephen, bowed down by consuming grief and melancholy, sought to rid himself of his agony by keeping his wife alive through writing his book. His obsession with her and with it is apparent. Stephen here demonstrates remarkable powers of sublimation, in that he is able after only one fortnight of grieving to begin the transformation of his sorrow into a work of art. It is my opinion that Virginia Woolf not only inherited her father's great gift of sublimation, but that his creative style of self-healing served as a model for what is perhaps her greatest book, *To the Lighthouse,* in which she too mourned the loss of and overcame her "obsession" with her mother.

I believe that Virginia's illness, in this instance, was precipitated by the fact that her lover, Vita Sackville-West, left her to go to Persia. Bell states (Vol. 2, p. 117) that "Virginia felt as a lover feels—she desponded when she fancied herself neglected, despaired when Vita was away, waited anxiously for letters, needed Vita's company and lived in that strange mixture of elation and despair which lovers—and one would suppose only lovers—can experience."

In a state of mourning, the loss of a loved one frequently resuscitates earlier griefs and induces us, to quote Shakespeare, to ". . . weep afresh love's long since cancelled woe" (Sonnet 30). I believe that the loss of Vita set off a mourning process in Virginia that brought back to consciousness the death of her mother. At that time, following her father's example, Virginia was able to use her genius to sublimate her sorrow in creativity. This process culminated in the working through of her grief in the great work of art, *To the Lighthouse*.

We have demonstrated many times that Leslie Stephen's difficult character structure played an important role in the development of Virginia's illness. We have also shown that his active encouragement of her intellectual development and identification with him was seminal in the evolution of her literary genius. It now becomes apparent that because of his gifts for sublimating his grief in creativity, he served as a major role model for Virginia in dealing constructively with despair. Thus he played a role as significant in the development of her genius as for her psychosis.

LESLIE AND VIRGINIA: A NATURAL EXPERIMENT IN HEREDITY AND ENVIRONMENT

Perhaps in the Stephen family we have an experiment of nature which can cast some light on the mystery of how the appalling disease of manic depression silently selects its victims, while permitting other people seemingly at similar risk to slip through its grasp.

As discussed in Chapter 1, mental illness was quite prevalent in the Stephen lineage, having struck down, in varying degrees, Leslie's first child and Virginia's half sister Laura, and Stephen's father, brother, and nephew. According to Hill (1979, p. 3), father and daughter "resembled each other physically; both were tall and gaunt, with wide eyes starting from a thin face, with fine, elegant hands, and with long, narrow legs and thighs that strode restlessly across the downs of Southern England. Both were temperamentally high-strung, Virginia seeming to have inherited her father's 'thin skin' in similar manner that Leslie Stephen inherited a thin skin from his father before him." Hill also states (ibid., p. 12) "And Virginia was so much like Leslie at age eight—a middle child, overshadowed by older siblings, sickly, very nervous, with a constitutional sensitivity to language. Leslie always referred to her with the same protective pity in his voice that he used for descriptions of his own childhood—he called her "my poor little Ginny." According to Love (1977, p. 15), "the possibility of his having passed on to her some genetic predisposition to emotional problems must be acknowledged, for Virginia's temperament and health resembled those not only of her father, but of her father's father as well . . . She said that she had inherited her 'secondhand' nervous system from her father and grandfather."

So here we have two individuals, seemingly at similar genetic risk, one of whom is a depressive personality, and the other a psychotic manic-depressive. Let us try to explore the fateful difference between them that enabled Leslie to lead the life of a relatively normal family man, albeit with "nervous collapses"; that fateful difference that condemned his daughter Virginia from the age of thirteen onward to many years of psychosis, as well as a sexless, childless marriage (Spater & Parsons, 1977, p. 177). If we can assume for the moment that father and daughter had inherited a similar propensity for manic depression (and of course, there is no way at present that we can do more than conjecture), we must look to a comparison of their early experiences to try to understand that "fateful difference."

Four factors present themselves as of possible importance in the differential diagnoses. The first concerns the age and probable manner in which Virginia was weaned. Love (1977, p. 214), cites an unpublished letter written by Leslie Stephen to his wife, in which he refers to her health and gives his consent for her to wean Virginia, who was then ten weeks old. In the light of Mrs. Steven's narcissism (Wolf & Wolf, 1979) it seems likely that Virginia's weaning was a shattering one, in which the emotional loss of her mother was even more traumatic than the untimely loss of the breast.

Stephen, in contrast to his daughter, seems to have been an overindulged child rather than a deprived one. We don't know, of course, when he was weaned, but knowledge of his early upbringing gives us some hypotheses to go on. For example, Annan states (1984, p. 16): "His mother spoiled him. Leslie was her favorite. His delicacy made him irritable, and in fact he had throughout his life a flaming temper. Years later his sister-in-law recollected some story of Leslie hurling a flower-pot at his mother and his family being astonished that no one seemed to be able to control him." In the light of such information, it seems unlikely that the infant Leslie suffered the untimely dissolution visited upon his little Virginia at the age of ten weeks. If these speculations are correct, we can surmise that a genetic predisposition to psychosis in Virginia was strengthened by a fragmentation of her ego at the time she was weaned, a calamity Leslie Stephen apparently was fortunate enough to escape.

The second factor in Virginia's developmental history which I believe contributed to that "fateful difference" was her circuitous path through the separation-individuation process. As we know from Chapter 1, her mother's presumed emotional unavailability during the rapprochement stage left Virginia incapable of affecting an age-adequate reconciliation during that potentially curative period.

Leslie Stephen, on the other hand, seems to have navigated the rapprochement crisis quite well. Remember, he was his mother's favorite, and apparently not subjected to the narcissistic distancing experienced by Virginia. In adult years, he kept in regular contact with his mother, and always felt emotionally close to her. As late as thirty years of age, during his religious crisis, when Stephen became a declared agnostic and resigned from his donship at Cambridge, he was able to "go home to mother." For Virginia there was no "going home." In contrast, Stephen was able to live with his mother until he married Minny two years later. When his mother died quite late in his life (he was forty-two), Stephen felt "as though I had lost an arm or a leg." Yet he didn't become psychotic then (or, for that matter, when Minny died later in the same year). Virginia, on the other hand, experienced her first manic attack on the death of her mother.

Third of all, Stephen's success in separation individuation prepared him well for dealing with the resolution of the Oedipus complex. Leslie Stephen, "his mother's darling," apparently could do no wrong. Supportive in all ways, it is likely that she was as present for him during the fearful urges of the oedipal period as she was at earlier stages. Although his father was a strict and religious man, it was said of the older Stephen (Annan, p. 8) that "Behind frowning providence God hid a shining face." The support of this relatively benign pair apparently enabled little Leslie to integrate the conflicting urges of the oedipal period. For Virginia, however, the oedipal period was fraught with danger. In contrast to her father's experience, Virginia's emotional difficulties were compounded rather than alleviated at the oedipal stage.

The fourth and perhaps most important "fateful difference" concerned the respective ages of Virginia and Leslie when their mothers died. Virginia was thirteen, Leslie forty-two! Virginia had no mother to help steer her through the vagaries of adolescence, to help her experience a psychological rebirth during that critical period of life known to some as the "second chance" (Blos, 1967). Leslie, on the other hand, lost his beloved mother long after he had happily replaced her with a cherished wife.

When we look at these four factors contributing to the "fateful difference" between the emotional health of Virginia Woolf and that of her father, Leslie Stephen; age and manner of weaning, success in navigation of both the rapprochement and oedipal crises, and the ages of death of their respective mothers, it appears that Virginia lost her mother at four critical periods when Leslie did not. When we also consider that between the ages of thirteen and twenty-two Virginia lost her half sister Stella, her brother Thoby, and Stephen himself, as well as her mother, the difference between the early histories of father and daughter becomes so salient that one must wonder whether in this case we need to consider the biochemical factor at all.

SUMMARY

Leslie Stephen, the father of Virginia Woolf, was a cacophony of contradictions. From all accounts, he was a bully, a manipulator, and a blustering, pessimistic, emotionally dishonest man. Although he could be lovable, charming, whimsical, encouraging, and deeply devoted to his family, he subjugated them to exploitation and abuse, demanding almost total abnegation of self. Julia Stephen, in contrast, was an optimistic, seemingly selfless person, who characteristically presented herself in an "up" mood to the world. Virginia incorporated both parental moods into her character structure. Therefore, it is postulated that pessimism and habitual deflating affronts on the part of one parent, in combination with a compulsive "good mood" on the part of the second parent, are a particularly lethal combination of character traits, which may contribute to the rapid mood shifting characteristic of manic depression in their offspring.

Unlike his wife, Stephen was a presence who could not be sidestepped. This combination of sweet and monstrous attributes in her father's nature and again in the contrasting temperaments of the parental couple must have been impossible to integrate for the small Virginia, who already was desperately engaged in the struggle for selfhood. She could not complete her development on the oedipal level, although she loved her father dearly, because identification with her mother meant further threat to an already weakened identity. Virginia's solution was to identify with her father in his character, his sexual identity, and his profession. Stephen was particularly devoted to Virginia, whom he regarded as an extension of himself; he encouraged this identification and served as her teacher and mentor. In that sense, he truly was the captain of the ship in her voyage *To the Lighthouse,* master of the currents that swept her onward to the grand light of her genius.

A fourfold comparison of Virginia Woolf and Leslie Stephen is made concerning their respective ages of weaning, success in navigating both the rapprochement phase of separation individuation and the oedipal period, and the ages at which their mothers died. Virginia lost her mother at four critical periods when Leslie did not. As a result, although father and daughter in a genetic sense resembled each other uncannily, it seems unnecessary to postulate a biochemical factor as the major "cause" of Virginia Woolf's manic-depressive illness.

3

Leonard and Virginia
"The Coward and the Snob"

*E*arly in her career, Virginia Woolf wrote (1978, p. 10): "I sometimes fancy that the only healthy condition is that of doing successful work. It's the prime function of the soul." Leonard Woolf was instrumental in helping Virginia carry out the "successful work" of her Stephen heritage. It was as her helper she needed him, but never as her mate.

Despite, or perhaps because of the fact that they had very different needs, Virginia and Leonard Woolf were a successful couple. Their needs were complementary, each compensating for the shortcomings of the other. Together they formed a complete unit. For example, Virginia was an individual who lived in a world of sensation and instinct, who was described as "all accelerator and no brakes." Leonard, on the other hand, was a compulsive, highly controlled individual who undoubtedly experienced vicarious satisfaction from Virginia's spontaneity and creative accomplishments. He served as her superego throughout the marriage, helping Virginia to control her impulses and maintain her self-esteem. Thus he protected her from severe psychotic episodes for 26 years, and together they became the literary genius known to the world as Virginia Woolf.

While Leonard had power over Virginia's everyday activities, ostensibly to protect her from insanity, Virginia seemed to wield power of another sort over her husband. Leonard, who had felt the least loved of his siblings by his mother, came from a Jewish family socially inferior to the Stephens. He probably accepted Virginia's high-handed treatment of him in part because she was his entrance ticket into the prized literary world of Bloomsbury (Ozick, 1983, p. 41). His low self-esteem apparently left him unable to protect himself from Virginia's abuse. According to Leonard himself, he was a coward and Virginia was a snob. Thus she was able to write with amused detachment that because of "the accident of his being born a jew" the "poor devil" was sentenced to a life of servitude as her husband. The Woolf marriage appeared to repeat the "pecking order" of the Stephen union: both hierarchies of power were based on prejudice. Stephen's bigotry was sexual, while Virginia's was racist.

Virginia generally was able to disguise her hostility at Leonard's tyranny during her well periods. Nevertheless it managed to "sneak through" at moments until it erupted with full force at the height of her manic episodes.

It is evident that Leonard was a marvelous helper for Virginia, and nurtured her career to its Olympian heights. As long as Virginia's creativity remained the primary goal of the marriage, the union was highly successful. But when Leonard apparently grew weary of functioning as Virginia's ego, he criticized her book, *Roger Fry.* Did this puncture her fantasy of ruling over the perfect "kingdom" and render her unable to control her rage against him? For Leonard was only her partner, and never really her husband. Nevertheless, I believe that the withdrawal of his emotional support of her writing recapitulated earlier losses in Virginia's life and was one of the primary factors that led to her insanity and death.

Leonard the Superego

The differences between the Woolfs' personalities both complemented their need for each other and shook up Virginia's psyche to the depths of her being. In Chapter 1 it was stated that in manic-depressives two superego functions fail to develop adequately: the ability to control impulses, and the capacity to regulate self-esteem. Examples were given of how little Virginia already suffered from "storm clouds" and "purple rages" as early as the nursery, and how the adult Virginia was famous 'for an uncontrollably caustic tongue. Evidence was also presented concerning Woolf's deficits in self-esteem, her nagging need for approval in the eyes of others, and the dreadful agony she experienced each time one of her works was published.

Leonard, on the other hand, was "all superego." According to Spater and Parsons (1977, p. 108), "he was not only a demanding taskmaster, but was inclined to doubt both the facts and the judgment of others, even on matters of minor importance, yielding only to the most incontrovertible evidence. Put more crudely, he was opinionated, he was stubborn, and he enjoyed argument. That he was usually right (and enjoyed being proven right) did not ease the problem of working with others. In controversy with his subordinates he was capable of working himself into a rage . . . which did not endear him to the objects of his rage." He frequently was petty, as well. For example, "On one occasion, anxious to prove that Angus Davidson was late, he insisted that they go out and check their watches, which varied by two minutes, against the huge clock that hung over the door of Pitman's School in Russell Square."

A compulsion neurotic, Leonard wrote down and catalogued everything he could. For example, each day he counted and recorded the number of words he had written (Spater & Parsons, 1977, p. 80), adding up to 61,649 words for his book, *The War for Peace*. His notebooks accounted for literally every penny spent on himself and Virginia. He noted in a private code detailed accounts of her menstrual cycles and daily mental condition. According to Spater and Parsons (p. 158), for 50 years Leonard recorded such divergent facts as the first frost of winter, elapsed time for driving from Monk's House to Tavistock Square, the number of miles he drove each year, the date he had his hair cut, the number of bushels yielded by each tree in his orchard, the outcome of every game of bowls he played with Virginia, and the principal events of the day. Apparently he legislated the actions of Virginia into his neurotic system as consistently as if they were his own. Ostensibly, this was done to ensure her health and productivity.

Leonard indicates that this was the role of all men as he saw it, and that he came by his values naturally. In his autobiography (1960, p. 15), he discusses the character of his paternal grandparents Woolf and says, "Yes, it was all, no doubt, as it should be—the male forbidding and the female forgiving. . . . The look of stern rabbinical orthodoxy in my grandfather's face was, I think, no illusion, for traditionally his family was just like that." That his superego derived from his paternal great-grandmother as well is suggested by Leonard as he continues:

"His mother, my great-grandmother, we were told, used to walk to synagogue with hard peas in her boots in the evening of every Day of Atonement until she was well over seventy, and she stood upright on the peas in her place in the synagogue for twenty-four hours without sitting down until sunset of the following day, fasting of course the whole time. Such behavior in the Woolf family about the year 1820 was considered to be the proper way to atone for your sins. I feel a faint sneaking agreement with my great-grandmother . . ." stated the husband of the feminist Virginia Woolf.

Much as Leslie Stephen played the role of "the cold bath" in the Stephen family, Leonard served as puncturer of Virginia's dreams, as well as the controlling functions of her ego. According to Virginia's niece, Angelica (Garnett, 1985): "Her [Virginia's] brilliance was not without malice, and her eyes shone with delight at her success. While her mind seized on the unconscious, weaker and more vulnerable aspects of people, noticing details of behavior with a brilliant haphazard appropriateness that skirted the edge of the possible, Leonard would wait, and then describe the same incident in terms that were factual, forthright and objective."

Not surprisingly, earlier in his life, Leonard had played the role of dream puncturer with his mother as well. In his autobiography (1960, p. 34), he tells us that his mother "lived in a dream world of rosy sentimentality and unreality." Family rows, which were infrequent, were "nearly always caused by one of her children disturbing my mother's dream." Leonard was the primary "disturber of the dream," as he informs us in the autobiography:

"She loved all her nine surviving children, but she loved me less, I think, than any of the eight others, because she felt me to be unsympathetic to her view of the family, of the universe, and of the relation of the one to the other." It is evident that Leonard knew that his "unsympathetic views" caused hostility, but apparently it never occurred to him that his sadistic character trait may well have contributed to his marital difficulties. One of Virginia's rare moments of conscious hostility to Leonard is captured in her diary (Vol. 4, 1982). "L. is very hard on people; especially on the servant class. No sympathy with them; exacting; despotic . . . His extreme rigidity of mind surprises me; . . . his severity; not to myself but then I get up & curse him . . . What does it come from? . . . His desire, I suppose, to dominate, Love of power . . . it is in private a very difficult characteristic. I must now get rid of Mabel, & find another." Virginia's niece, Angelica Garnett, gives us further information on the superego aspect of Leonard's character in her book on growing up in Bloomsbury (1985, p. 53):

"One of the rare but regular events was tea with Leonard and Virginia. Virginia I knew would treat me as a special person—almost as Vanessa did. Leonard, however, was another matter, and was the only member of the family who could successfully refuse me something I wanted, whose very tone spelt the finality of real authority, against which there was no appeal. He was dispassionate, and perhaps it was the perception of a different attitude which, while it impressed me, made me vacillate, unsure of what I want or why." Garnett adds: "I felt the austerity of their lives compared with ours . . . Virginia and Leonard's work allowed them only just time for a frugal meal; preoccupied with thoughts of the 'New Statesman' or the House of Commons, Leonard encouraged no elbows on the table, cigars or liquors—he was off, like a secretary-bird, to more gripping occupations."

Corroborating the image of Leonard as the benevolent tyrant, Garnett states (p. 113) that Leonard never was able to "hide his brief anxiety that Virginia might drink a glass too much wine or commit some other mild excess; he would say quite simply, 'Virginia, that's enough,' and that was the end. Or, when he noticed by the hands of his enormous watch that it was 11:00 in the evening, no matter how much she was enjoying herself, he would say 'Virginia, we must go home.' "

According to Bell (1972, p. 32), who understandably considered Leonard the family saviour, Leonard was cast in the "ungrateful role of family dragon.'' For example, it was impossible for Virginia to resist and Leonard not to resent the trooping in of her sister Vanessa's children. It fell to Leonard to see that Virginia did not have too many guests, or that the ones she had did not stay too long. Here again, Leonard took over a normal ego function, that of self-assertion, which he felt Virginia was incapable of exercising.

So here we have a married couple in which one partner was inordinately gifted in the ability to enjoy the sensate world, albeit deficient in certain ego and superego functions which left her unequipped to exist in the world of reality, while the other was burdened with a severe superego that enabled him to function but unquestionably impaired his ability to enjoy life. The marriage was indeed a working, well-functioning *folie à deux* which benefited both partners although it undoubtedly infantilized Virginia and kept her in a dependent position.

Let us take a further look at the manner in which Leonard served as Virginia's symbiotic partner. As previously stated, he monitered her actions constantly, deciding when she was able to see friends, go to parties, or be shipped off to bed. It was Leonard who decided that Virginia was incapable of handling a child, and who made the rounds of physician's offices until he found one who agreed with him, a decision for which it is unlikely she ever forgave him. He had absolute charge of the purse strings, doling out to Virginia what he deemed a suitable (if niggardly) amount of spending money. Can we suppose this incurred her wrath innumerable times per day? It was Leonard to whom Virginia came with each manuscript when it was finished: Only after he had read and approved of it was she able to relax. And it was Leonard to whom Virginia came to ease the daily ''slings and arrows of outrageous fortune'' to which she was inordinately heir. For example, in his autobiography (1967, p.149), Woolf states: ''We used to say that Virginia was continually picking up mental thorns—worries which she could not get rid of—particularly from criticism. She would come to me and say: 'I've got a thorn,' and we would discuss the thing until we had got the thorn out.''

Thus we see a wife dependent upon her husband for daily functioning. Leonard assumed the responsibility of preserving Virginia's sanity as if it were part of himself. According to Hinsie and Campbell (1977, p. 446), "in mania, the ego for a time has thrown off the yoke of the superego and protests, 'I don't need control anymore.' The removal of inhibition allows all those impulses (mainly oral) which had been kept down to come to the fore." I believe that when Leonard feared that Virginia's superego was not strong enough to control her impulses, he stepped in and picked up the deficit. As a result, she remained relatively well after her major breakdown in the early years of their marriage without a serious attack of mania for 26 years. But both partners must have paid dearly for this policing action. For who among us would not resent our jailer? And what warden is not the captive of his prisoner? And so they made each other pay.

HER BREAKDOWN

Early in her marriage Virginia Woolf suffered the longest and most acute emotional breakdown of her life. She was ill for almost three years, with one remission of several months' duration, and tried at least once during this period to kill herself. Indeed, her sister and family were afraid she never would be well again. If one were to read only Virginia's diaries and the words of her family (i.e., Bell, that marrying Leonard was the wisest decision she was to make in her lifetime), one might be inclined to wonder why, during the honeymoon of this "happiest of marriages," the bride would suffer the most severe breakdown of her life. To seek to understand the origin of Virginia's total collapse, it behooves us to turn to the similarly "happy" union of Rachel Vinrace and Terence Hewett in Woolf's first novel, *The Voyage Out* (1915), published by Virginia's half brother George one year after her recovery.

In the novel, the heroine, Rachel Vinrace, an isolated innocent of twenty-two with a strong need for autonomy, travels on her father's ship *Euphrosyne* (Joy) with her aunt and uncle. The aunt, who has decided to teach the motherless young woman how to behave in society, succeeds in getting Rachel to become attached to Terence Hewett, who makes a declaration of love and marriage to Rachel. After accepting him, Rachel develops a fever, becomes delirious, retreats into a coma, and finally dies.

According to Leasks (1979, p. 329), Rachel needed "to avoid attachments which put her imagined freedom in jeopardy." "Why did he make these demands on her?" Rachel asks as Terence tries to get to know her. "Why did he sit so near and keep his eye on her? No, she would not consent to be pinned down by any second person in the world . . . I like walking alone, and knowing I don't matter a damn to anybody . . . I like the freedom of it . . ." (p. 215). Yet when she provokes Terence into retreating, as did Virginia's mother during the rapprochement period, Rachel becomes depressed. What Rachel wishes above all else is to feel loved and cared for, while allowed at the same time to maintain her autonomy. But she does not believe such love is possible, for it is completely out of her experience. She has never learned to cope with the blinding force of love without the danger of losing herself. In the delirium of her illness, Rachel found herself walking through a tunnel under the Thames, thus symbolically returning to the great mother-womb in death. "She fell into a deep pool of sticky water, which eventually closed over her head," wrote Woolf (p. 341). "She saw nothing and heard nothing but a faint booming sound, which was the sound of the sea rolling over her head," curled up at the bottom of the sea.

Rachel Vinrace's escape into death, like that of Virginia's half sister Stella, was the only way she knew to resolve the conflict between the wish to be loved and the need to preserve her autonomy. Unlike Virginia's, Rachel's hallucinations were not effective enough to save her. Only in death could she find peace. On the other hand, Virginia Woolf was somewhat stronger than either her heroine or her half sister Stella. For Virginia was able to find in psychosis a compromise measure which enabled her to preserve her selfhood from Leonard's domination and at the same time remain under his care. That her "post-honeymoon psychosis" was the most severe of a lifetime indicates that at this period Virginia Woolf was living out the central problem of her life. That she eventually came out of her psychosis suggests that in some part of herself she felt ready to face the conflict while sane. Through psychosis, creativity, and later the gratification of her love affair with Vita, Virginia succeeded in warding off death until her mature years. Then she, too, took the route to peace she had unknowingly predicted 26 years before with the death of Rachel Vinrace—escape under the waters with only "the sound of the sea rolling over her head."

THE COWARD AND THE SNOB

We have discussed the Woolf marriage in respect to Virginia's need for Leonard. Now the question arises as to what Leonard got out of the union, once he got past his enchantment with her beauty. Several possibilities come to mind. First and foremost, Leonard was a writer, but a far less talented and successful writer than his wife. A realist like Leonard must have recognized that he was not a genius, and that by nurturing Virginia's ability he vicariously could share in her achievements. Secondly, there is the matter of his compulsivity. As previously stated, he was a man who lived frugally in the emotional as well as financial sense, with a minimum of spontaneity and instinctual pleasures. He probably found vicarious satisfaction in identifying with Virginia, who lived in a world of sensation and fantasy. If so, by lending himself to the marital symbiosis Leonard regained a long-lost part of himself. She the instinct, he the control, the two together added up to one whole.

Bell states (1972, Vol. 2, p. 94) that Leonard needed Virginia "in moments of pain and disappointment." But it seems to me that the most important element for Leonard in maintaining the marriage concerns his lifelong insecurity, I have stated earlier that Leonard believed that of the nine children in his family he was the one his mother loved least. It is feasible that Leonard, regarding himself as unlovable, in masochistic fashion felt that the enormous drain upon his emotions and health that came with being the mate of Virginia was the price he had to pay to feel loveworthy. If this idealized creature could love him, then surely he was worth being loved; it would prove his mother was wrong, and his wounded self-esteem would be healed.

Although Leonard came from an intelligent family, including a barrister father, they never reached the heights of literary aristocracy achieved by the Stephens, "the finest grain of the finest station in England" (Ozick, 1983, p. 48). According to Spater and Parsons (1977, p. 59), "the cultural gap between the Woolf and Stephen families [was] not the difference between Reformed Jew and agnostic Christian, but that between the professional middle class and the cultured and leisured upper class intellectual." Since Leonard wanted to be a writer, it is likely that the Stephens represented the kind of family to which he wanted to belong, and to which his own clan seemed inferior. When Leonard as an undergraduate at Cambridge became friendly with Virginia's brother Thoby (p. 180–183), and later, when he met the illustrious Leslie Stephen, Leonard confessed in his autobiography that "Thoby's family seemed to a young man like me formidable and even alarming." And when he met the Misses Stephen—Virginia was eighteen or nineteen—he felt that they "were just as formidable and alarming as their father, perhaps even more so." Leonard's comparison between the Woolf and Stephen families may well have been exacerbated by the fact that Virginia never really liked his mother, and indeed, made frequent fun of her. For example, Virginia said of Mrs. Woolf at the age of 84 that she was "spry as a weasel," and wrote that "Work and love and Jews in Putney take it out of me" (Bell, 1972, Vol. 2, p. 4). Another time (1977, p. 6) she commented that "I do not like the Jewish voice; I do not like the Jewish laugh: otherwise . . . there is something to be said for Flora Woolf [Leonard's sister]."

"And how did the Woolves regard her?" Bell asks (p. 3). "Did they perceive that she thought their furniture hideous? Did she seem to them a haughty goy thinking herself too good for the family of their brilliant son? I'm afraid that they probably did." Bell's feelings of conflict between daughter-in-law and mother-in-law are borne out by the fact that Leonard's mother did not attend their wedding.

But the most important aspect of Leonard's insecurity, it seems to me, concerned his religious background. At the time of their marriage (1912), anti-Semitism was rampant among the British upper classes, and unfortunately, Virginia's attitude toward the Jewish people was representative of her class. "There are a great many Portuguese Jews on board, and other repulsive objects, but we keep clear of them," she wrote to Violet Dickinson (1975, p. 184) from somewhere off the coast of Spain seven years before her marriage took place. When Leonard was courting her, she wrote him (Bell, 1972, p. 185): "I feel angry sometimes at the strength of your desire. Possibly, your being a Jew comes in also at this point. You seem so foreign." In a later letter to Violet Dickinson (1975, p. 500), Woolf wrote, "I've got a confession to make. I'm going to marry Leonard Woolf. He's a penniless Jew." The fateful effect of her anti-Semitism on their relationship (surprising in an atheist and feminist far ahead of her time) was well expressed by Virginia (Spater & Parsons, 1977, p. 172), in the following anecdote in which she described the difficulties of travelling from city to country before the days of automobiles: 'My husband presides with considerable mastery—poor devil, I make him pay for his unfortunate mistake in being born a Jew by discharging the whole business of life." It is my opinion that Virginia's statement typified the balance of power in the marriage. Virginia bullied Leonard, treated him as a subordinate or servant, and justified this because of his "inferior" status. Leonard, feeling insecure in Virginia's love, accepted the role of underling because he felt he had to, in order to keep her as his wife. As Woolf insightfully stated in his autobiography (1960, p. 100), "I used to tell Virginia that the difference between us was that she was mentally, morally, and physically a snob, while I was mentally, morally and physically a coward—and she was inclined to agree."

The final factor in attempting to understand what Leonard got out of the marriage concerns his literary pretensions and his wish to be accepted by Bloomsbury. According to Ozick (1983), what Leonard needed the most in Virginia Woolf was not her genius but her madness. She believes that Leonard's seriousness, his "uxoriousness," would have been totally unacceptable to the high excitement and frivolity that characterized Bloomsbury, that Leonard's compulsive personality would have been a "drag" which would certainly have made them reject him as a member. But Virginia's psychosis was the ticket that admitted Leonard into the society. "It used his seriousness, it gave it legitimate occupation, it made it both necessary and awesome . . . It was his wife's insanity in short that made tenable the permanent—the secure—presence in Bloomsbury of Leonard, himself. Her madness fed his genius for responsibility; it became for him a corridor of access to her genius. The spirit of Bloomsbury was not Leonard's, his temperament was against it—Bloomsbury could have done without him. So could a sane Virginia."

The marriage of Virginia's parents apparently served as a model for the Woolf union, and greatly contributed to its neurotic structure. In the Woolf household Virginia played the role of her father and Leonard that of Julia, Stephens' long-suffering wife. The stance of underling in both marriages was based upon the supposed inferiority of one individual to another. In the case of the Stephens, the pecking order was based on gender, for in the last quarter of the nineteenth century, "everyone knew" that women were the inferior sex. In the marriage of Virginia, the pioneer feminist, and Leonard, the political liberal, the status hierarchy had shifted to a foundation of religious background instead of sex. As Rose stated it (1978, p. 88), "She managed to turn the tables on Victorian patriarchy." But she did so by substituting one form of bigotry for another.

THE ASEXUAL MARRIAGE

Another unanswered question about the marriage of "the Woolves," as they were known, concerns their lack of a sexual relationship. According to Gerald Brenan (Spater & Parsons, 1977, p. 177), in whom Virginia apparently had confided, the couple lived "chastely," except for a few abortive efforts early in the marriage. Like Clarissa Dalloway (Woolf, 1925, pp. 45–46), Virginia spent her conjugal nights in her "virginal narrow bed."

"Like a nun withdrawing, or a child exploring a tower, she went upstairs . . . There was the green linoleum and a tap dripping, there was an emptiness about the heart of life; an attic room . . . The sheets were clean, tight stretched on a broad white band from side to side. Narrower and narrower would her bed be . . . lying there reading, for she slept badly, she could not dispell a virginity . . . which clung to her like a sheet. Lovely in girlhood, suddenly there came a moment—for example on the river beneath the woods at Clieveden—when, through some contraction of this cold spirit, she had failed him. And then at Constantinople, and again and again. She could see what she lacked. It was not beauty; it was not mind. It was something central which permeated; something warm which broke up surfaces and rippled the cold contact of man and woman, or of women together. . . . She resented it, had a scruple picked up Heaven knows where, or as she felt, sent by Nature (who is invariably wise). . ."

In *Mrs. Dalloway* (p. 14) Woolf describes the terror of loss of self that sentences Clarissa to her conjugal "narrow virginal bed": "But often now this body she wore . . . this body, with all its capacities, seemed nothing—nothing at all. She had the oddest sense of being herself invisible; unseen, unknown; there being no more marrying, no more having of children now, but only this astonishing and rather solemn progress with the rest of them. . . . this being Mrs. Dalloway; not even Clarissa anymore; this being Mrs. Richard Dalloway." To avoid complete loss of identity, then, Virginia Woolf, like Clarissa Dalloway, sentenced herself to a marriage without sex. "I don't like profound instincts—not in human relationships," Virginia wrote (*Letters*, 3, p. 366).

GEORGE

Virginia's family had a different "explanation" for her frigidity. A favorite theory of the "Virginia Woolf Industry," much touted by Bell (1972) and even Virginia herself, is that her half brothers abused her sexually. It is widely believed that Gerald "fondled and exposed her private parts" when she was a child of six, and that George came into her bed and caressed her after her mother died. As a result, the half brothers, in particular George, are held responsible for Virginia's frigidity with Leonard. This supposition lets Leonard and the marriage off the hook and perpetuates Leonard's sainthood. To me, however, this "explanation" does not hold up psychologically.

Suzanne Henig (1973, pp. 57–59), editor and cofounder of the *Virginia Woolf Quarterly*, and famous Woolf scholar, also contests the "George theory of frigidity." According to her, the charges of child molestation leveled against George were grossly unsubstantiated, and were made in England at the time of the publication of Bell's biography in order to "have a titillating scandal guaranteed to make it an instant commercial best-seller." Henig reminds us that Bell frequently stressed the unreliability of Virginia's versions of the truth. Yet he was quick to accept without any satisfactory documentory evidence "the notion that George Duckworth, a man whose many kindnesses and solicitations both Virginia and Vanessa continually accepted even after the purported sexual advances, was a sexually maladjusted individual whose particular vice was incest." Henig adds "If George . . . were alive today, the unproven statements related by Bell would be actionable in the English courts; but under British law, one can libel the dead without incurring such actions. No one truly knows whether George did or did not molest the young Virginia and Professor Bell's alacrity in espousing this notion without any real evidence and then attributing Virginia's sexual frigidity and lesbianism to it as first cause is psychological nonsense." It is also interesting that no one seems to question why Vanessa, who is said to have been subjected to the same molestation by George, became neither frigid nor a lesbian.

Were frigidity such as Virginia's to follow this kind of sex play, it could be due only to earlier developmental difficulties which would have resulted in grave sexual problems in any event. Thus Virginia's frigidity with Leonard, in line with her deepest pathology, seems to be a function of the early fear of engulfment that she first experienced during the rapprochement phase of separation-individuation and which was exacerbated by the fear of identifying with a mother who lost her life in marriage.

This opinion seems corroborated by the character of Sara, in *The Years* (Woolf, 1937), who had been dropped as a baby and, as a result, suffered a crippled shoulder. While her sister Maggie goes to a dance, Sara has to stay home and lie in bed (pp. 136, 146). Sara's physical handicap surely stands for the emotional crippling undergone by Virginia, who wrote in her diary (1982, p. 148), "I hardly know which I am, or where: Virginia or Elvira" (who became Sara in *The Years*). Virginia, too, had been "dropped" by her mother, at the rapprochement phase of development. The fact that Sara's injury occurred in infancy also suggests that the time of origin of Virginia's psychological illness occurred long before the so-called molestations by George and Gerald. While her sister Vanessa, like Maggie, "danced" (was sexually active), Virginia literally had to lie in bed, either to avoid a further breakdown, or to convalesce. Sara found compensation in her injury, however. Although her sexuality was maimed by the crippling, the handicap brought her closer to her mother, who, like Mrs. Stephen, could love only those in need. Woolf, the novelist, astutely observes that when Mrs. Pargeter made a remark to Sara, she was "smiling at her daughter whom she loved perhaps because of her shoulder" (p. 141). "We cannot help each other," says Sara's brother, North, "we are all deformed" (Woolf, 1937, p. 380).

The fact that Woolf used autobiographical material extensively in her writing also confirms Henig's view. I know of no work of Woolf's that hints at any such scenes as were purported to have been perpetrated by George. The exhibitionist's exposure seen by Rose in *The Years* (pp. 26–42), which caused such deep shame in her that she was unable to tell her secret even to her big sister Eleanor, often is spoken of as analogous to the "George" episodes. But, to my mind, such an occurrence is a different experience altogether. Rose's traumatic encounter with nakedness would be far more likely than the purported fumblings with her stepbrothers to contribute to the formation of a character like Virginia's. The victims of exhibitionists often are detached "lookers and watchers," objective observers like the narrator in so many of Woolf's books. Yet, for them, looking is eroticized and with Virginia they tend to expose in others what they would keep hidden. Such individuals, however, usually are conflicted about their voyeuristic activities, no matter how benign their actions, and may experience considerable guilt because looking has become associated with the unconscious pleasure experienced in childhood while glancing at the forbidden genitalia. Guilt at such an experience could have contributed to her frequent breakdowns at the conclusion of her novels. For a detailed report of her "peeping" and exhibitionism was recorded publicly for all the world to "see."

In *The Voyage Out* (1915), the chaste young heroine Rachel is kissed by an older man, Richard Dalloway. Although she later has a terrifying nightmare of being trapped in a vault with a deformed man with the face of an animal, her first reaction is to be seized with a "strange exaltation . . . Life seemed to hold infinite possibilities she had never guessed at" (p. 85). It was not only the sexual pleasure which terrified Virginia, but also her fear of being trapped. "I felt weak, you see," she said in describing the

"assault" to Helen, in an earlier typescript of *The Voyage Out.*
"I felt he could do what he chose with me" (as quoted by Rose,
1978, p. 55).

Similarly, the sexual "abuse" with George, if it occurred at
all, may have been as much a source of "strange exaltation" to
Virginia as it was to Rachel Vinrace. For example, Bell tells us
(1972, p. 79) that on one social occasion Virginia's drawers fell
down while she was saying goodbye to her hostess. Finding
George at home in the drawing room, she "flourished the errant
garments in his face." It is also interesting that Bell reports that
"George was speechless with indignation." Be that as it may, it
is likely that Virginia's stepbrothers had little influence on the
overall scheme of her sexuality. For Virginia never overcame her
terror that "The long white tentacles that amorphous bodies leave
floating so they can catch their food, would suck her" (*The Years,*
1937, p. 377). And Leonard accepted his sexual deprivation too
soon and too easily.

LEONARD'S REWARD

Again, what did Leonard get out of the arrangement? Why
did a presumably normal able-bodied man put up with the denial
of his deepest instincts? Let us examine once more Leonard's
character, as well as his sexual history (Woolf, 1960) in an attempt
to answer these questions.

First of all, we have seen that Leonard's severe superego
served as the primary component of his character structure.
Strictness of superego is the most important way in which compulsion neurotics ward off instinct. As one whose "austere life"
left time only "for a frugal meal" (Garnett, 1985, p. 53), it is difficult to picture Leonard as an individual bursting with uncontained
sexual passions. Rather, I suspect that Virginia's asexuality was
compatible with her husband's preferred way of life.

In line with this thinking, Leonard was still a virgin at the
age of twenty-five. Despite his professed "sexually tormented and
tortured existence" between the ages of twelve to twenty-five, it
appears characteristic of him that he brought about neither a
change in the sexual patterns of his marriage nor an alteration of

his sexual status in adolescence. According to him (1960, p. 82), as a boy, "Love and lust, like the functions of the bowels and bladder, were subjects which could not be discussed or even mentioned. The effect of this was . . . a buttoning up of mind and emotions." I suspect that this "buttoning up" was the major defense used in dealing with sexual deprivation in his marriage, just as it served as the tool for his deprivation in adolescence.

When Leonard was a boy, he attended St. Paul's on a scholarship, and lived at Arlington House. Here, according to Woolf (p. 66), the nature and problems of sex were explained in lurid and minute detail "by a small boy who had probably the dirtiest mind in an extraordinarily dirty-minded school. I was at the time completely innocent and I had considerable difficulty in concealing from him the fact that it was only with the most heroic effort that I was preventing myself from being sick." To a typical compulsion neurotic, the sexual act is contaminated by the proximity of the sexual organs to the organs of excretion. That the child Leonard shared similar ideas is suggested by his comparison of love and lust with the functions of the bowel and bladder. Therefore, it is likely that Leonard Woolf, compulsion neurotic par excellence, had sexual problems of his own before he married Virginia; that, in all probability, he considered sex "a dirty act," and did not wish to "soil" his delicate virginal bride. Hence he gave in rather too readily to his new wife's aversion to sex because it suited his own superego. Thus Leonard was able to say (1960, p. 79):

"It would be difficult to exaggerate the instinctive nastiness of human beings which is to be observed in the infant and child no less than in middle or old age. To call it original sin is absurd, for it would mean that we accept as true metaphysical fairy tales or religious nightmares. It is safer to recall and state the hard facts without inventing explanations like the Platonic ideas, Allah, Jehovah, or Jesus Christ. The fact is that at age of ten, I was a fully developed human being, mean, cowardly, untruthful, nasty, and cruel, just as I was at twenty, fifty, and seventy." I do not believe that Leonard was any more guilty of these "sins" than the rest of us; only it is truly tragic he believed that he was. As a result, he was unable to spare himself or his wife the sad effects of such self-denigration.

UNDERGROUND RUMBLINGS

Virginia Woolf, in a burst of enthusiasm about her life with Leonard, once said, "I daresay we are the happiest couple in England" (Bell, Vol. 2. 1972, p. 71). Many different sources of material entitle us to cast a suspicious eye upon her declaration of happiness. Virginia herself wrote that "every secret of a writer's soul, every experience of his life, every quality of his mind is written large in his works" (Spater & Parsons, 1977, p. 83). Hence we can do no better than to look at certain of her short stories to understand the underlying truth of the Woolf marriage. Her raging behavior toward Leonard, and her total rejection of him for as long as two months at the height of her manic attacks, cast further doubt upon the validity of Virginia's declaration. Suspect also is her need for a lifelong love affair with Vita Sackville-West, and the fact that less than a year after her honeymoon with Leonard, she made her first attempt at suicide by taking a lethal dose of veronal (opus idem, p. 67). And finally, there is the indisputable fact that as Leonard's wife, Virginia succeeded in taking her own life.

Important indications of a pathological relationship with her husband are contained in Woolf's last published stories. For example, *Lapin and Lapinova* is a short story finished by Virginia two years before her death (Woolf, 1939, pp. 68–78). The story opens with the marriage of Mr. and Mrs. Ernest Thorburn. Four days later, the bride wonders if she will ever get used to the fact that she is Mrs. Ernest Anybody. She realizes she does not like her husband's name, which suggests her mother-in-law's dining room in Porchester Terrace. When it occurred to her that he did not look so much like an Ernest as a rabbit, the two devise a shared lapidary fantasy which makes them laugh merrily together. But a grim foreboding of the future rears its head. "But how long does such happiness last? they asked themselves; and each answered according to his own circumstances" (p. 69).

Whenever they had nothing to do or talk about, which apparently was often, the bride allowed her fantasy to play with the story of the Lapin tribe. "He ruled over the busy world of rabbits." She was not so lucky, for "her world was a desolate, mysterious place, where she ranged mostly by midnight. All the same, their territories touched; they were King and Queen" (p. 70–71). "Without that world, Rosalind wondered, that winter could she have lived at all?" Thus lived Virginia Woolf, too. According to Leonard (Woolf, 1963, p. 232), "All day long, when she was walking through London streets or on the Sussex downs or over the water meadows or along the river Ouse, the book would be moving subconsciously in her mind or she herself would be moving in a dreamlike way through the book." This inner world of Virginia's, like that of Lapin and Lapinova's, was shared by Leonard Woolf (1977, p. 73), who totally immersed himself in "the busy world" of nursemaid and publisher in order to live out the shared literary fantasy. According to Virginia (1977, p. 73), "Both agreed that life seen without illusion is a ghastly affair."

But, back to the Lapidary kingdom. There came the day of the golden wedding party of the parental Thorntons (p. 72), which Rosalind dreaded. "As she walked upstairs she felt bitterly that she was an only child and an orphan at that, a mere drop among all those Thorntons assembled in the great drawing-room with the shiny satin wallpaper and the lustrous family portraits. . . . No, she was not happy. Not at all happy. She looked at Ernest, straight as a ramrod with a nose like all the noses in the family portraits; a nose that never twitched at all . . . As the dinner wore on, however, the room grew steamy with heat. Beads of perspiration stood out on the men's foreheads. She felt that her icicle was being turned to water. She was being melted; dispersed; dissolved into nothingness; and would soon faint." Rosalind protected her identity by escaping into a world of fantasy, as Virginia protected hers by immersion into the world she created in her books. When her denial by fantasy (A. Freud, 1946, pp. 73–88) failed, that mechanism "of denying the existence of objective sources of anxiety and pain" (p. 85), Rosalind fell apart, as did Virginia at the end of every book, when she had to face harsh reality alone.

One day when Ernest came home from work to their "nice little home; half a house above a saddler's shop in South Kensington, not far from the tube station," Lapinova asked her king what he thought had happened to her that day as she was crossing the stream. "What the deuce are you talking about?" he responded. That night Lapinova slept badly. "In the middle of the night she awoke, feeling cold and stiff, as if something strange had happened to her. Turning on the light at last she looked at the husband lying beside her. "Was it possible that he was really Ernest; and that she was really married to Ernest?" she wondered. A picture of her mother-in-law appeared before her eyes, on their golden wedding day. She could see herself in the same position fifty years hence, and found the thought unbearable. Ernest woke up, and seeing her sitting bolt upright beside him asked what the matter was. "I thought my rabbit was dead," she whimpered. "Don't talk such rubbish," Ernest responded. "Lie down and go to sleep."

But there was no more sleep for the diminished Lapinova, whose protective membrane had been ripped away from her. "Next day she could settle to nothing. She seemed to have lost something. She felt as if her body had shrunk; it had grown small, and black and hard . . . The rooms also seemed to have shrunk. . ."

After a long time Ernest came home, "Oh, Ernest, Ernest . . . it's Lapinova," she cried wildly. . . . She's gone, Ernest. I've lost her." Ernest frowned, and then pressed his lips tight together, and after ten seconds answered, "Oh, that's what's up, is it? . . . Yes . . . poor Lapinova . . . caught in a trap . . . killed." Then he sat down and read his newspaper.

Woolf then comments, "So that was the end of the marriage." I believe she was talking about her relationship with Leonard as well. It seems to me that every marriage has a motif, whether it be child rearing, pleasure, amassing a fortune; and the dominant theme of the Woolf union was the development and flowering of Virginia's genius. Because Leonard was a realist, he must have known that her talent surpassed his; therefore he all but gave up his own writing career until after her death in order to devote himself to nurturing Virginia's talent. As such, he "became doctor, nurse, parent, semi-husband, and chief literary adviser" (Spater & Parsons, 1977, p. 70). He even became a publisher in order to spare Virginia the trauma of having her manuscripts criticized by insensitive publishers. If the goal of the marriage was Virginia's literary development at all costs, then the union, if not "the happiest in all of England," was remarkably successful in carrying out its long-term goal. But was it really a marriage? If one accepts that the book *Orlando* (1928) was autobiographical, Virginia herself seems to have had misgivings about her marriage (p. 238): "She was married, true," Orlando mused, "but if one's husband was always sailing around Cape Cod, was it marriage? If one liked him, was it marriage? She had her doubts."

But as with Lapin and Lapinova, it seems a truism that one person can carry out another's fantasy life only so long without becoming resentful at the loss of identity (Bond, 1981). As earlier noted, the year before Virginia took her life, Leonard criticized a book of hers (*Roger Fry*, 1940) for the first time, thus puncturing the dream they had shared so long. Just as Ernest shattered his wife's fantasy, Leonard, the "dream puncturer," destroyed Virginia's inner world in which two individuals had merged to make the dream of one come true. While Lapin's "mistake" brought about the end of his marriage, Leonard's defection, by reenacting the early criticism of her mother and the "cold bath" of her father, helped bring about the end of Virginia's life.

Another of Virginia's short stories, *The Legacy*, written at the end of her life, and published posthumously (1921), possibly casts further light on the Woolf marriage. The story concerns still another couple, the Clandons, in which a self-absorbed, insensitive husband is unaware of the dissatisfactions experienced by the wife. In this case, the husband is mourning his spouse's death from an automobile accident. It is only in reading her diary that he discovers that she has been unfaithful to him, that her lover has killed himself, and that her death has been a suicide. "He had received his legacy," Woolf ended the story. "She had told him the truth. She had stepped off the kerb to rejoin her lover. She had stepped off the kerb to escape from him."

Why two stories in the same period of time in which the wife cannot bear her husband, and must escape? In the one case she turns to fantasy, in the other suicide. In the first story, *Lapin and Lapinova*, we see how Virginia identified with the heroine in turning away from her real husband to a fantasy world. Is Virginia telling us in the second story that when her fantasy escape failed she felt she had no recourse but to turn to death? If the story is autobiographical, we should look to her diaries for further enlightenment. Ah, but we really can't. For Leonard Woolf has so censored the diaries that it is impossible to find anything in them unflattering to *him*. David McCullough tells us (1985) that "One of the most interesting things about autobiography is what the author leaves out . . . If they're leaving it out, it's probably very important." Since there is no way of finding out the secrets Leonard "left out," it remains for us to follow Virginia's advice that every secret of a writer's soul is written large in his works and search out the psychological meaning in her writings. And what this psychologist finds "writ large" is that Virginia Woolf killed herself in part to escape from her husband.

If Leonard's "defection" punctured Virginia's fantasy world, why did she take it so hard? What traumatic incidents in her past did Leonard's action recapture that were traumatic enough to cause her breakdown and death? To understand this (as with a patient in analysis) we must hark back once more to Virginia's early history and try to ferret out the causes of these catastrophes.

LEONARD: THE "BAD MOTHER"

We have offered evidence in Chapter 1 that her mother provided a particularly rich symbiotic period of life for Virginia, which Mrs. Stephen severed prematurely for her own narcissistic needs. For many years, Leonard, too, served as a "good mother" to Virginia. He considered her creative needs primary, and shielded her from the onslaughts of the world. Yet when Leonard, for his own reasons, needed to end the illusion of eternal availability, Virginia responded much as she must have at four or five months of age, with a complete emotional collapse.

One of Virginia's earliest memories took place in her bedroom at St. Ives, where, left alone in a strange setting, she felt wrapped in a golden membrane. I would presume that, without her mother's presence, the terrified infant found protection from fright by regressing to a womblike state. In my opinion, Leonard's maternal protectiveness of Virginia's career provided another golden membrane which served to protect her from total mental collapse for 26 years. That this ego function, which in the ordinary course of infancy develops as a result of adequate mothering, was given over to Leonard, is corroborated by Virginia (1977, p. 70) after a brief separation from her husband:

"But I was glad to come home," she wrote, "and feel my

real life coming back again—I mean life here with L. Solitary is not quite the right word, one's personality seems to echo out across space, when he's not there to enclose all one's vibrations. . . . the feeling itself is a strange one—as if marriage were a completing of the instrument, and the sound of one alone penetrates as if it were a violin robbed of its orchestra or piano."

This paragraph indicates that Virginia lacked adequate ego boundaries, and therefore was not aware of where she ended and the world began. In addition, she probably was born lacking that healthy "stimulus barrier" with which normal infants are equipped to shield them from being overwhelmed with too much stimulation (Freud, 1920). According to Leonard (1967, pp. 52–53), "A curious thing about her was that, although she was extremely sensitive to noise and was one of those people who 'jumped out of her skin' at a sudden noise or unexpected confrontation, she seemed usually, when writing, to acquire a protective skin or integument which insulated her from her surroundings." This impairment, which may well be the original defect contributing to the manic-depressive psychosis, is again indicated in her diary (1977, p. 71) when Virginia complained ". . . of the clamour and blare of military music and church bells which always takes place at about 11—a noise which other people have no right to inflict." Virginia's mother apparently was unable to help the sensitive child to cope with surplus stimulation. For many years Leonard helped Virginia to compensate for this emotional deficit by "enclosing all her vibrations." When he finally criticized her work, she was left overwhelmed with the pain of her "mental thorns," pain she was unable to "enclose" alone. As a result, 58 years after her experience at St. Ives, Virginia lost her "good" mother once more.

LEONARD AND LESLIE

The second precipitating cause for Virginia's breakdown was Leonard's "betrayal," which must have been experienced by Virginia as a repetition of the loss of her father. Leslie Stephen was Virginia's intellectual mentor. He served as her teacher and encouraged her development as a writer. This ongoing association with her prestigious father was a vital growth experience in Virginia's life. It helped her to individuate from a relatively amorphous relationship with her mother and permitted her to be close to her father in a constructive nonsexualized manner. Thus she was able to carve out her own niche in her father's world. As Stephen's undisputed favorite, she won out over both mother and siblings, including her "baby brother," Adrian. Stephen's approval of her writing was crucial to Virginia's mood, as indicated by a dream from her letter to Clive Bell a few months after her nephew Julian was born (1975, p. 325): "I dreamt last night that I was showing father the manuscript of my novel; and he snorted, and dropped it on a table, and I was very melancholy, and read it this morning, and thought it bad."

This dream probably was precipitated by Virginia's dependence on Clive Bell, her sister's husband, after Vanessa's baby, Julian, was born. Her liaison with Clive suggests that Virginia turned to her father for support after her brother Adrian was born. Like many little girls, Virginia probably fantasied that she and her father inhabited a special kingdom together. This fantasy may have been paramount in helping her to maintain a precarious adjustment during her growing-up years. When reenacted with Leonard as the "good father," the gratification possibly served to fuel Virginia's writing career for 26 years. When Leonard burst the bubble, it cost Virginia her "good" early mother, her loving oedipal father, and her own special mentor. She was left to face that she, like Lapinova, was married to a stranger she hated. This *folie à deux* between Virginia and Leonard had worked better than most "acting-out" solutions, for it produced a glorious "brainchild," the genius of Virginia Woolf. Nevertheless, in keeping with the repetition compulsion (Freud, 1919, part 111), in which the organism tends to repeat traumatic events, the collapse of Virginia's fantasy left in its wake a bereft, inconsolable child.

FURTHER DISSATISFACTIONS

We have seen how the Woolf marriage was symbiotic, with each participant seeming to complete the personality of the other; one plant, one whole, as Virginia said in her *Sketch of the Past* (1976, p. 71). Leonard was a controlling man in every aspect of

Virginia's life, from each mouthful she ate to the number of minutes he permitted her to devote to her writing. Virginia, mistrusting her own sanity, invariably obeyed Leonard's commands. Surely a woman who required "a room of her own," with a reputation based in part on her resentment of male authoritarianism, would object to Leonard's domination. It seems likely that the feminist doctrine of *A Room of One's Own* (1929) and *Three Guineas* (1938) was inspired partly by a revolt against Leonard, as well the entire male sex.

In Chapter 2 we showed how Julia Stephen lived in typical Victorian bondage to her husband; we indicated how this arrangement wreaked havoc on the opportunities for growth and development in both partners. According to Lilienfeld (1981, p. 151), Virginia and her sister Vanessa "smashed the patriarchal superstructure of marriage as Leslie Stephen enforced it; and reworked the emotional mode of the marriage bond." This may be true of the Woolf marriage in terms of career and health, but in the moment-to-moment decisions of the household, such as having a friend to visit, taking a walk, or staying up late of an evening, Leonard was absolute dictator; his word was law. When one looks at the power structure of the union, in which Virginia found it necessary to "steal" a few extra moments past 11 o'clock at a party, it is difficult to agree that the "patriarchal superstructure of marriage" actually was smashed at all.

That the Woolf marriage left much to be desired is evident in Virginia's behavior during her manic episodes. The torrent that erupts during psychotic episodes is fueled by rage that has been repressed during other periods of the individual's life. Virginia's total rejection of Leonard at these times suggests great hostility toward her husband which she managed to squelch during her well periods. At the height of her psychotic episodes the rage ruptured its barriers; Virginia ranted and cursed Leonard and refused to see him for as long as two months at a time.

HER "HONEYMOON PSYCHOSIS"

Virginia and Leonard were married on August 10, 1912. As early as December of the first year of marriage, Bell notes (p. 227) that she was "unwell with headaches." Virginia's health remained poor, with headaches and insomnia. She became increasingly depressed and in July entered a nursing home. Her depression, delusions, and resistance to food increased. In September she attempted suicide. She recovered temporarily, but in April and May of 1915, had another breakdown, "the most violent and raving months of her madness." According to Bell (1972, p. 24), "she entered into a state of garrulous mania, speaking ever more wildly, incoherently and incessantly, until she lapsed into gibberish." A month later, she displayed "even more harrowing symptoms, for now Virginia was violent and screaming, and her madness culminated in virulent animosity towards Leonard himself." Three months later, her sister Vanessa wrote that Virginia "won't see Leonard at all and has taken against all men." This breakdown of Virginia's was the worst she experienced in her lifetime. Not a good recommendation for the first three years of a marriage; the prognosis for its future did not seem bright.

As we have noted, it is well known that rage experienced during psychotic episodes is fueled by anger that has been repressed during other periods of life. Certain evidences of Virginia's hostility to Leonard during her "normal" periods "sneak through" his editing of her work. For example, five years after they were married, Woolf wrote (1977, p. 59): "We were rung up and asked to dine with the Bells in Soho, and this, I regret to say, led to much argument; we put off going to Kingston; the night was wet, and L. didn't want—old arguments in short were brought out, with an edge to them." These "old arguments," according to Bell's footnote, "concerned VW's thirst for social life and LW's anxiety lest she should over-strain or excite herself." It is also informative that when Leonard insisted that Virginia leave their hosts precisely at 11 P.M., Virginia showed her hostility by taking "a few extra minutes stolen from beneath his nose" before she was able to rise and reluctantly follow Leonard to the door (p. 34).

Eleven years into their marriage, in a mood of depression, Woolf wrote (Bell, 1972, p. 89): "Never pretend that the things you haven't got are not worth having . . . Never pretend that children, for instance, can be replaced by other things." Here Woolf expresses her sorrow that she never had children, a decision which she held against Leonard all her life. Unable "to venture against his will" and express her rage fully, she turned the anger against herself, and experienced psychosomatic symptoms of headaches and the "jump in her heart." Thus she got revenge on Leonard, because her "ill health" spoiled his pleasure. Not so different from the Stephen marriage, in which Julia was unable to express anger and took psychological revenge on her husband as did her daughter decades later.

In similar vein, two years later Virginia took off for a week in France alone with Vita Sackville-West. According to Bell (1972, p. 139), "On the morning of their departure the journey caused a small and sudden row between husband and wife." Then Leonard, equally spiteful, got his revenge by not sending Virginia any news of himself. This alarmed her enough to send a telegram to Leonard to ensure that all was well.

But perhaps the ultimate word on the Woolf marriage is undisguised in Virginia's final work, *A Summing Up,* the last story in the posthumously published book entitled *A Haunted House and Other Short Stories* (1949). In it (pp. 147–148), Woolf's counterpart Sasha asks herself of life, "Which view is the true one?" A tree accidentally supplies her with the answer. "But what answer?" she asks. "Well that the soul—for she was conscious of a movement in her of some creature beating its way about her and trying to escape which momentarily she called the soul—is by nature unmated, a widow bird; a bird perched aloof on that tree." This story suggests to us that at the end of her life, Virginia recognized her true identity. The tree is a phallic symbol representing her father. Virginia, "by nature unmated," in the depths of her soul was "a widow bird" in mourning for her father. Her real self is identified with Leslie Stephen, who is perched on the heights he yearned for and never quite attained.

SUMMARY

Despite, or perhaps because of the fact that they had very different needs, Virginia and Leonard Woolf had a workable marriage. Virginia lived in a world of sensation and instinct, while Leonard was a compulsive, highly controlled individual, who undoubtedly experienced vicarious gratification from Virginia's creativity and spontaneity. He served as her superego throughout the marriage, helping her to control impulses and maintain her self-esteem. Thus he protected her from severe psychotic episodes for 26 years, and enabled her to become the literary genius known to the world as Virginia Woolf.

The difference in their needs, while contributing to a workable marriage, also led to a power struggle between the couple. While it is documented many times over that Leonard had almost complete control of the details of Virginia's daily life, to which she often objected, this was only part of the power struggle between them. In his compulsive way, Leonard unquestionably was the victor, whose spoils included complete command of the household. He could get away with this because she was terrified of madness, and felt Leonard could keep her sane. Virginia's victory, on the other hand, was a psychological one. She once wrote that Leonard "had the misfortune to have been born a Jew," and often treated him as a high-class servant. Leonard came from a Jewish family who were lower on the socioeconomic scale than the Stephens, and had also been the least loved of siblings by his mother. Thus he came to his marriage with a deeply ingrained sense of inferiority. As a result of this sense of unworthiness, he was unable to protect himself from Virginia's psychological abuse. It is interesting that Virginia's marriage followed the script for dominance–submission written by her parents, in that both marriages were based on supposed evidence of superiority–inferiority. In the Stephens' marriage the "pecking order" was based on sex; in the Woolf household the basis was racial, as well as the state of Virginia's health.

Sexual aspects of the marriage are also discussed. It is hypothesized that Virginia, like her "chaste" heroine, Mrs. Dalloway, needed to refrain from sex with her husband in order to maintain her separateness. In addition, sexual withholding was another victory for Virginia in the power struggle between the couple.

One must also inquire as to why Leonard put up with this sexual deprivation. In response one must look at his sexual history. He was a compulsion neurotic, one of a group who characteristically consider sex a filthy and perverse act. Leonard's early history as given by himself in his autobiography bears out this diagnosis. Therefore one can postulate that Virginia's sexual frigidity fit in with his idealization of her, and was compatible with the style of life deemed acceptable by his severe superego. The supposed advances of Virginia's half brothers are not considered by this writer of primary importance in the etiology of her illness. Although Virginia seemed to meekly obey Leonard's dicta, it is suggested that this did not sit as well with her as her family thought. Outbursts of hostility to Leonard occasionally broke through her defenses, especially during her manic periods when they erupted crudely, intensively, and vociferously. At their height she refused to see her husband at all.

The writer believes that Leonard really helped Virginia maintain her sanity for long periods, and even further was instrumental in nurturing her career to its pinnacle. He protected her from many of the petty annoyances of life so that she was free to devote herself to writing, to the point where he founded a publishing company to safeguard her from the pains of rejection and editorial stress frequently encountered by writers. The marriage thus was a developmental one, which helped Virginia to function in the world in a limited sense and to achieve her major life goal. The symbiosis was successful as long as Virginia's career was of central value to Leonard. But when he became critical for the first time of one of her books, *Roger Fry, A Biography,* she became despondent and no longer was able to keep her despair under control. The loss of Leonard's support recapitulated early losses in Virginia's life, and undoubtedly contributed to her psychosis and suicide.

Monk's House, Rodmell

Talland House, Saint Ives

Monk's House, Rodmell

Monk's House, garden side

4

Vanessa

"The Cure That Failed"

VANESSA'S ROLE IN VIRGINIA'S WORLD

When Virginia Stephen turned away from her mother during the rapprochement stage of separation-individuation, she looked to her sister Vanessa for substitute mothering, and this continued for each subsequent crisis of her life. By and large, however, Vanessa proved an unsatisfactory substitute.

Such a crisis occurred on the death of Sir Leslie. Virginia experienced terrible grief at that time, "something feverish, something morbid, something which made her feel isolated and afraid" (Bell, 1972, Vol. 1, p. 88). In addition, she found herself emotionally drained and exhausted by the seemingly interminable months of his illness. She was thus a prime candidate for her ensuing breakdown.

Vanessa, on the other hand, had experienced the death of her father quite differently. As the person mainly responsible for his life and household after the death of her half sister Stella, Vanessa had felt tied down and burdened. On Sir Leslie's death, she was plainly delighted at regaining her freedom, and being released from the care and ill temper of this tyrannical man. Under the circumstances, Vanessa obviously was not able to be much of a consolation to the grieving Virginia. While recuperating from her breakdown, she wrote to her friend, Violet (1975, p. 147): "Nessa contrived to say that it didn't much matter to anyone, her included, I suppose, whether I was here or in London, which made me angry, but then she has a genius for stating unpleasant truths in her matter of fact voice!" Since it is particularly painful to observe the good fortune of another when one is in deep despair, Virginia found Vanessa's happiness impossible to bear. Bell stated that he felt that Vanessa's indifference to Virginia's state of mind contributed to her grief and subsequent mental breakdown. At the death of Sir Leslie, then, Virginia lost both her father and her sister, the two people closest to her. Bell's speculation is borne out by the fact that during her psychotic breakdown, it was Virginia's mistrust of Vanessa, as well as grief for her father, that became "maniacal" (Bell, Vol. 1, 1972, pp. 88–89), and that Virginia shrieked out with long stored-up rage.

In 1913, after her first year of marriage and the completion of *The Voyage Out* (1916), Virginia experienced the gravest emotional breakdown of her life. She always became depressed, and often emotionally ill, when she finished one of her novels. Virginia's characters filled her, kept her company round the clock, during the writing of her novels. She often talked aloud to them night and day, whether she was in the bathtub, walking about the downs, or striding down the Strand. So long as she was writing a novel, Virginia Woolf never felt alone. Like many artists, however, every time she finished an important work she went into mourning, feeling as empty and bereft as if she had suffered the death of a loved one. As usual, when Virginia was most desperate for mothering, Vanessa needed to protect her own autonomy. Ostensibly, the sisters became estranged this time over the renting of Asheham, the Woolfs' first country house. Virginia had let the house in August, and Vanessa was furious because she wanted the house for herself and her friends. Virginia responded with silence, and her condition deteriorated. Vanessa sensed her part in her sister's failing mental condition, and once more expressed her concern and guilt to Roger Fry. It was then that with more rationalization than honesty she wrote (Bell, Vol. 2, p. 13), "Oh God, I can't help being rather worried lest I ought to have done more, but after all one cant do much with married people."

According to Virginia (1978, p. 159), early in the year that she and Vita met, the sisters had become estranged again. As usual, Vanessa had felt the need to separate, and wrote in her diary that she did not expect to see her sister until May, since she was going abroad. Virginia not only missed her sister, formerly the love of her life, but her absence left a space Virginia was unable to fill. "I felt a sort of discontent," she wrote, "as the door closed behind her. My life, I suppose, did not vigorously rush in." Thus it seems that Vanessa's defection left Virginia "wide open" for the advent of a new love to fill the empty space within.

By failing to fill the role of mother that Virginia required, by not being psychologically present for her at the death of their father, Vanessa was woven into the fabric of Virginia's second major breakdown. By not being emotionally available to Virginia at the completion of her first novel, Vanessa indirectly helped to precipitate Virginia's homosexual love affair.

It is interesting that for a few months before and after Virginia's love affair with Vita began, no letters passed between the sisters. It appears that there was a cooling off between Virginia and Vanessa because of the latter's jealousy. Vanessa did not often deign to express her need for Virginia or to admit her jealousy of Vita's other loves, but so jealous a creature was Vanessa that, according to Kushen (1983, p. 69), Virginia's absence in Greece with Leonard, and Roger and Margery Fry in 1932, "brought Vanessa to complain of the separation and to bridle with jealousy of the Frys." If this is true, then Bell's statement (1972, p. 13) can be paraphrased to say that Vanessa's jealousy and resulting indifference to Virginia's pain contributed to her grief and subsequent suicide. Once more, Virginia had lost not one love but two. Without emotional support, it was too much to bear.

On July 20, 1937, a great tragedy occurred that temporarily bridged the estrangement between the sisters. Julian Bell, Vanessa's twenty-nine-year-old son, was killed as he drove an ambulance during the Spanish Civil War. Virginia came immediately to her sister's side, visited her at least twice a week during her convalescence, and remained her great solace and comfort during the nightmarish period of mourning, which was even more of a horror because it was a repetition for both women of the earlier trauma of their brother Thoby's death. Vanessa took to her bed, and Virginia, as was her wont when facing despair, quickly regressed to her infantile self. She was able to do very little work. Letters between the sisters were now quite frequent, and Virginia's style reverted to that of the yearning child. For example, less than a month after her nephew's death, a needy Virginia wrote her sister (1980, p. 5): "I wish dolphin [Virginia's pet name for her sister] were by my side, in a bath, bright blue, with her tail curled. But then I've always been in love with her since I was a green eyed brat under the nursery table, and so shall remain in my extreme senility." On August 8 (1980, p. 155) she wrote: "I long— oh why are you the only person I never see enough of?—to see you again." And again in August (p. 156) she responded breathlessly: "Yes, I'll come to tea tomorrow, my own darling creature. You shan't be rid of me for long. In fact I cant bear not seeing you."

Shortly thereafter, Virginia sent out even more urgent messages (1980, p. 157), writing Vanessa: "My love for you has always been fuller than your thimble," and (p. 158) "I rather think I'm more nearly attached to you than sisters should be—why is it I never stop thinking of you?" In the same letter she stated she felt about six and a half years old. This poignant cry for help was followed by (p. 177) "You can't think how I depend upon you, and when you're not there the colour goes out of my life, as water from a sponge; and I merely exist, dry, and dusty."

During the following year, probably because Vanessa's pain made her more emotionally available to her sister, Virginia's need for Vanessa seemed to abate. Letters between the two became less frequent and fervent, as Virginia's piteous pleas diminished.

By October 24, 1938, Virginia's letter to her sister (1980, p. 294) indicates that once again all was not well. She describes an almost overwhelming impulse to join Vanessa abroad, which she said she resisted partly because she understood Vanessa's need for autonomy. But it seems far more likely Virginia resisted such urgency because she knew she would be unwelcome. "I very nearly rushed off to Cassis," she wrote, "so intoxicating were your words; and the sense of heat; and vines; and beauty; and freedom; and silence; and no telephones. You very nearly had me on you; and then what a curse you would have found it! . . . your perfect globe would have been smashed; you know how careful I have to be, too, to bait my hook with little minnows [sic] and other tidbits to disguise my rapacity for your society with whats acceptable to you." Virginia also desisted from obeying her "urge," according to her letter, because she and Leonard were so unhappy when parted, "the complete failure of our marriage prevented it," and her feeling that their need for separate identities made occasional separations necessary. "It's a good thing," she wrote, "that the Woolf's and the Bells should be separated sometimes in order that each may inspissate their identity."

I doubt that she really thought it was a "good thing." Rather, she said what she knew was "acceptable" to Vanessa. Kushen (1985, p. 87) believes that Virginia's desisting was a valiant gesture, an incredible act of intuition, which helped her "step back from the brink of a union disastrous to her own psychic health and survival." I do not agree. While her letters at this time are cheerful on the surface, I believe that Virginia's desperate need for her sister was an ominous symptom which heralded the recurrence of her deadly illness. She desperately reached out to the "good mother," Vanessa, to rescue her from the loss of her lover, from her disappointment at Leonard's reaction to *The Years,* from the stark fact that Hitler had invaded Czechoslovakia and that war was imminent, and from her grief for Julian, which evoked memories of the earlier loss of her brother, Thoby. She needed Vanessa to fill the developmental gap left by her mother's early withdrawal, to stop her precipitous fall into psychosis. Virginia urgently yearned for Vanessa because Vita was emotionally unavailable at this time, and Vanessa alone had the power to counteract her sister's headlong descent into disaster. Had Vanessa been able to put Virginia's needs before her own, and obviously she could not, bereft as she was by the death of her son, she might have wired, "Drop everything. Come right away." When Vanessa failed once more, I believe she struck one of the final blows that led to the death of Virginia Woolf.

After Vanessa's silent rejection of Virginia, their correspondence became less personal. According to Kushen, (p. 88), "Virginia was kept at arms length . . . gossip served to provide subjects for talk other than the personal. Vanessa and Virginia did not meet alone, but among friends. . ." During the next two years or so, the sisters wrote sporadically, mostly about Vanessa's (unaccepted) proposal that Hogarth Press publish Julian's literary efforts. Virginia attempted to maintain a superficial cheerfulness in her letters, but neither her emotional state nor the failing relationship healed.

As a result of her urgent neediness, Virginia was inordinately jealous of those she felt were more fortunate recipients of Vanessa's largesse. In this case, the target was Helen Anrep, Vanessa's friend and the former mistress of Roger Fry. Three years before, Virginia had pleaded with Vanessa (1980, p. 163), "[Do] you like Helen Anrep better than me? The green goddess, Jealousy alit on my pillow this very dawn and shot this bitter shaft through my heart. I believe you do." This time Virginia's jealousy led to a bitter impasse between the sisters, which had a tragic outcome. For it precipitated what amounted to a final break with both Vanessa and reality, and contributed to Virginia's "final solution" to her emotional difficulties.

The 1940 break again ostensibly came about through a real estate transaction. Vanessa had told Helen Anrep about some property to let in Rodmell. Virginia was inordinately enraged, even though Helen and her children lived there for only one week. Vanessa was not sympathetic, feeling that Virginia was "unnecessarily angry" at their coming. The quarrel between them was so serious that, save for a worried note posted to Virginia eight days before her death, no letters passed between the sisters the last year of Virginia's life. According to Kushen (1983, p. 99), "Virginia's inner sense of abandonment and desolation (was) overwhelmed at the Anreps' presence." Like a beggar child yearning for the cookie behind the bakery window, Virginia could not bear to see others getting what she desperately desired. To spare herself the pain of unfulfilled longing, and the humiliation of another rejection by her sister, "Slowly Virginia withdrew from the intolerable reality and the inner, internecine enemy raged."

VIRGINIA'S DREAM

When Virginia was thirty-seven years of age, she wrote a letter to her friend, Janet Case, in which she described a dream (1976, p. 378) that symbolically reveals the intricacies of Virginia's relationship with Vanessa, as well as with her mother. "I was dreaming about you so vividly last night," she wrote to Janet, "that I must write and find out whether this means that you were thinking with kindness of me. I'm afraid not. In my dream you were entertaining a Princess, and you wouldn't look at me— whereupon I flew into a rage, and turned to Emphie [Janet's sister] for comfort, and she was immensely grand, and made me feel myself so much in the way that I marched down the garden and out into the road, and left you bowing over the hand of your Princess. What can it all mean?"

This dream is interesting in the light of Virginia's emotional history as well as her lifelong relationship with Janet Case. Janet had been Virginia's Greek teacher, and the two had been very close friends. In fact, Janet had helped to take care of Virginia for several weeks in 1914 during the recovery from her breakdown. But for some time before the letter was written in 1919 there had been a considerable distancing between the women, so much so that in 1917 Virginia wrote Margaret Llewelyn Davies that Janet Case "has vanished into the past" (1976, p. 178). Twice, about that time, once before and once after the date of the dream, Virginia expressed her concern that Janet was quite critical of her novels. On Nov. 13, 1918, she wrote Vanessa (1976, p. 293): "I had a fearfully depressing talk with old Janet Case the other day; at the end of which I came to the conclusion that when nice educated people . . . have less feeling for modern fiction, including my own which she advised me to give up and take to biography instead since that was 'useful' . . . it's high time for us writers to retire to the South Seas." Even more ominously, in November, 1919, Virginia wrote in her diary (1977, Vol. 1, p. 313) of her resentment and fury that Janet totally dismissed her novels, as well as her emotional ability to feel what a writer should: "Janet and she [Margaret Llewelyn Davies] felt that perhaps—they might be wrong, but still in their view—in short my article on Charlotte Bronte was so much more to their liking than my novels. Something in my feeling for human beings—some narrowness—some lack of emotion—here I blazed up and let fly. . . . You grant that Janet moralizes? I said."

Here, then, we have Virginia furious with the once close but now distant and critical Janet, who in the dream is entertaining a Princess and "wouldn't look at" Virginia. Shades of Mrs. Stephen, who had been too preoccupied with her family duties and social activities to spare a moment alone with her little girl, the very mother who was highly critical of Virginia and whom we hypothesized had rejected little Virginia's first "productions." Criticism of her writing as an adult could well have been reminiscent of her mother's earliest disparagement. As a result of her pain and fury in the dream, Virginia in retaliation turned away from Janet as she had done with her real mother long before, and looked to Janet's sister Emphie for comfort, as she had turned to her own sister Vanessa in real life.

But as in real life, the sister from whom she wished comfort made Virginia "feel so much in the way" that she "marched down the garden and out the road." Janet's sister failed to replace the disinterested mother figure in the dream, just as Vanessa in a crisis was no more interested in Virginia than Mrs. Stephen had been. Virginia, who found it difficult all her life to admit that Vanessa made her "feel so much in the way," similarly wishes to deny that the friendship between herself and Janet is all but over. Although the letter ostensibly was written to find out whether the dream meant that Janet was "thinking of her with kindness," Virginia's comment, "I'm afraid not," indicates that on a deeper level she already knew the regrettable truth.

Thus the dream expresses Virginia's unconscious knowledge that neither her mother nor her beloved sister had any time for her, as well as the fact that her long-valued friendship with her mother-substitute, Janet Case, is all but over. Unable to bear the pain of losing yet another cherished one, and afraid that she would become depressed or insane, as she had done at the loss of her mother, Virginia tried in the dream to replace Janet with her sister Emphie, as she repeatedly had tried and failed to replace her absent mother with Vanessa. But, as in real life, the displacement is a failure. For the repetition compulsion (Freud, 1920) is silently at work in the dream, just as it is in life. Virginia at the age of thirty-seven had not yet mastered either the loss of her mother or the repeated disappointments with Vanessa. By replaying the traumatic family situation with Janet and Emphie as the new cast of characters, Virginia made another valiant attempt to master the major catastrophes of her life.

THEIR SADOMASOCHISTIC RELATIONSHIP

If Vanessa failed to meet Virginia's emotional needs for optimal psychological development, it is also true that each played an intense central role in the life of the other. From their earliest years onward, the relationship of the Stephen sisters was fraught with sadomasochism. As previously noted, when the girls were but toddlers in the nursery, Vanessa (and perhaps Thoby) had a technique for making Virginia "turn purple with rage." But even Bell, that champion of the Stephens family, concludes (1972, Vol. 1, p. 24) that his mother, Vanessa, surmised that "these paroxysms were not wholly painful to Virginia."

The terror, pain, and rage suffered by Virginia when taunted by her sister and brother Thoby is suggested by Woolf in *The Waves* (1931, p. 224) when Rhoda laments: "I shall fall alone through this thin sheet into gulfs of fire. And you will not help me. More cruel than the old torturers you will let me fall, and will tear me to pieces when I am fallen."

In my opinion, Vanessa's sadistic treatment of Virginia continued all her life as she masochistically sought Vanessa's love and Vanessa persistently withheld it. Their behavior toward each other as adults is aptly described by Virginia's niece and Vanessa's daughter, Angelica (Garnett, 1985, p. 107):

"Virginia, seeing myself and Vanessa sitting by the fire or under the apple tree in the garden, would crouch beside us, somehow finding a small chair or low stool to sit on. Then she would demand her rights, a kiss in the nape of the neck or on the eyelid, or a whole flutter of kisses from the inner wrist to the elbow . . . Virginia's manner was ingratiating, even abject, like some small animal trying to take what it knows was forbidden . . . After a long hesitation, during which she [Vanessa] wished that some miracle would cause Virginia to desist, she gave her one kiss solely in order to buy her off . . . Once Virginia had been liberated by receiving her allowance of kisses, she became detached, quizzical, gay and intimate. Vanessa, let off the hook . . . continued to feel waves of frustration and reserve; the hedge in which she sat, and which Virginia had been trying to break down, grew less thick and impenetrable."

Masochism and sadism abound in this paragraph. Virginia's masochistic stance is first suggested by her crouch and borne out by her abject, ingratiating manner. Feelings of unworthiness cause her to select an inferior position in regard to Vanessa, when Virginia symbolically selects the "small chair or low stool" to sit on. Then by "demanding" love she behaves in a way designed to force her sister to reject her (Bond, 1981), which of course she does. Vanessa, on the other hand, behaves as a typical sadist. In order to protect a weak sense of autonomy she spitefully withholds the love and approval her victim craves, experiencing sadistic pleasure in the bargain. Vanessa appears to have suffered from another typical weakness of sadists, as well, a lack of firm ego boundaries which frequently result in the inability to say "no" without resorting to drastic measures. Not wishing (at least consciously) to give affection to Virginia, Vanessa behaves badly to prevent herself from capitulating to the insistent Virginia. But to no avail; Virginia finally "wins." Since Vanessa is inhibited in the expression of her homosexual feelings, Virginia by her masochistic behavior is "helping" Vanessa to feel and express the genuine affection which lies beneath her wooden surface. As a result, Virginia is able to "penetrate the hedge in which she [her sister] sat" and thus enable the hedge to be "less thick and impenetrable." When Vanessa finally yields and gives Virginia what she desires, she quickly recovers. Through their sadomasochistic interaction both women eventually get what they need. Were Vanessa not restrained by her own pathology, she may well have given the affection Virginia craved without all the neurotic accoutrements. Given that her actions were excessive and inappropriate, had Virginia been less needy and able to wait instead of pressuring her sister, she may well have been given the affection Vanessa genuinely felt. This interaction seems patterned after that of the parental Stephen marriage in which Mrs. Stephen got revenge on her difficult husband by refusing to tell him she loved him.

Vanessa was seen by her sister as an uninhibited child of nature, as a creature of the wild, independent of the demands of civilization. And indeed Vanessa was remarkably free of many of the mores of her time, living, for example, with her unmarried lover Duncan Grant, often together with his homosexual lover, and and bearing Grant an out-of-wedlock child. Woolf wrote of Vanessa's clone Susan in *The Waves* (1931, p. 119), "She has the stealthy yet assured movements . . . of a wild beast. She seems to find her way by instinct in and out among these little tables, touching no one . . . yet comes straight to our table in the corner." Nevertheless, careful study of the relationship between Vanessa and Virginia makes it clear that Vanessa, despite her reputation for uninhibited heterosexuality, had grave sexual and emotional problems. Although she accepted Grant's homosexuality, awareness of her own was deeply repressed; nor was she cognizant of how provocatively she behaved to Virginia. Since she was unable to love her sister as deeply on the conscious as on the unconscious level, Vanessa helped maintain in its stead an intense sadomasochistic relationship. This deep sexual inhibition was acted out in her love life with a man as well, to her own detriment. As noted in *The Masochist Is the Leader* (Bond, 1981, p. 387), sadomasochists often have one relationship in which they play either the sadistic or masochistic role, while they simultaneously are involved in a "side" relationship of the opposite pole. Virginia, while subservient to Vanessa and Vita, was abusive to Leonard (see Chapter 3). Vanessa, on the other hand, lived most of her adult life with Duncan Grant, who treated her as badly as she did Virginia, causing her the same kind of pain by withholding his love. Vanessa spent their "married" life yearning for Duncan's love, while he tormented her with the presence of his homosexual lovers. This discrepancy in their availability for each other seems graphically illustrated by the size of their respective beds in Charleston: Vanessa had a narrow bed, reminiscent of Virginia's bed in Rodmell and the "chaste" bed of Mrs. Dalloway. Duncan, on the other hand, slept in a large-size bed meant for sleeping two. Obviously, if they were to make love at all, Vanessa had to be the aggressor who made the approaches to Duncan.

How aware were the sisters of their pathological interaction? Did Vanessa accept any responsibility for their difficulties, or did she place the blame entirely on her sister's "craziness"? We cannot know for certain; but it seems that Vanessa felt at least some guilt about her treatment of Virginia. For example, at the age of thirty-three, Vanessa confessed to Roger Fry her misgivings (Bell, 1972, Vol. 2, p. 8): "Virginia has been very nice to me. She saw that I was depressed yesterday and was very good—and cheered me up a good deal. Do you think I sometimes laugh at her too much? I don't think it matters, but really I am sometimes overcome by the finest qualities in her. When she chooses she can give one the most extraordinary sense of bigness of point of view. I think she has in reality amazing courage & sanity about life."

It is interesting that Vanessa is able to tell Roger Fry what she could not give to Virginia in person. Like many sadists, Vanessa was able to give her victim what she craved, so long as it was not demanded. In her letter of condolence to Vanessa after Virginia's death, Vita states that Vanessa had even told her to tell Virginia what she, Vanessa, could not: "I should like you to know," she wrote, "that (at your request) I did tell her [Virginia] what you had said about the comfort she had been to you over Julian, and I have never seen her look more pleased and also surprised. I know that your message gave her the keenest pleasure" (Spalding, 1983, p. 317).

I believe that Virginia was at least partially conscious of the deep, dark pleasures her sister experienced in withholding expression of her love, as she was later to be aware of the pleasure Vita experienced in causing her (Virginia) pain. In 1910 (1975, p. 429) Virginia wrote to Vanessa: "I fear you abuse me a good deal in private and it is very galling to think of it . . . as I never abuse you." But then, love-starved as she was, Virginia was quick to deny her knowledge, as she added: "But I dare say this is all great nonsense; and if it isn't, there may be no use in saying it."

Virginia's rage at Vanessa, while only partially conscious, came through at other times in her dreams. For example, on August 4, 1908, she wrote Vanessa (1975, p. 341): "I woke from a terrible dream, in which Jack [Hills] was breaking to me the news of your fatal injury from an omnibus. . ." This dream combines many functions. In addition to wishing to be rid of her frustrating as well as beloved sister Vanessa, Jack Hill was Virginia's half sister Stella's husband, who no doubt reported the news of Stella's death to the Stephen family. The dream is an effort to master the death of her half sister and, earlier, her mother, as well as expressing the fear that whom one loves one loses.

On August 8, 1909, showing another moment of insight concerning Vanessa's character, which was not always available to her on a conscious level, Virginia wrote her sister: "I dreamt all night that I was arguing with you, and you showed a peculiar bright malice, which I sometimes see in you."

Vanessa's inability to express affection to Virginia may well have stemmed from her earliest feelings of jealousy and rivalry. According to Kushen (1983, pp. 47–48), Vanessa was aware very early of their rivalry over their brother Thoby, for her "happy relation with her younger brother [was] rocked by Virginia's intrusion into the nursery paradise." Kushen continues, "Vanessa's failure to remember her feelings of jealousy as a child would indicate the painful and intense quality of these emotions and their very early preverbal or never verbalized experience as well as their rapid repression." Kushen then states that Vanessa was jealous of Virginia's relationship with Thoby as well as her looks and verbal ability, which made her very successful with adults. "She, as well as they, perceived her brilliance and beauty, particularly the loveliness of her coloring, green eyes and rosy skin." It was this repressed jealousy of Virginia which burst its bonds all their lives together, and caused Virginia innumerable hours of "sweet suffering" (Shainess, 1984).

THE "CURE" THAT FAILED

When little Virginia found her mother unavailable, she turned to her siblings in the nursery, in particular Vanessa, to protect her from the vagaries of life without a mother. So great was Virginia's desperation that she took whatever love Vanessa offered, no matter how dubious the package. In this sense Virginia's masochism, distorted as it was, can be regarded as her means of seeking a "cure" for her developmental deficiencies. The intensity of her need was stated by Louis in *The Waves* (1931, p. 96) when he said: "For I am the weakest, the youngest of them all . . . I am always the youngest, the most innocent, the most trustful. You are all protected. I am naked." Vanessa, jealous of the intelligent and lovely child who was beloved of the adults and intruded into her exclusive relationship with Thoby, tormented her little sister mercilessly (Bell, 1972, Vol. 1, p. 24). The more Vanessa tortured Virginia, the more desperate Virginia became in the attempts to make her sister love her.

Because of her own problems with jealousy and autonomy, Vanessa in a psychological sense treated Virginia badly. Like Louis in *The Waves* (1931, p. 142), "Pain and jealousy, envy and desire, and something deeper than they are, stronger than love, and more subterranean" was uppermost in the relationship. For the sadomasochistic relationship between the sisters was piercingly strong. The administering and acceptance of pain, the struggle of Vanessa to withstand Virginia's forceful demands and the occasional yielding to them, remained a powerful emotional tie. The interplay between them was exciting and sensual and filled the inner emptiness left by an absent mother. For the two lonely children, even a painful relationship was better than none at all. "I grasp, I hold fast," said Susan, Vanessa's counterpart (p. 228). "I hold firmly to this hand, any one's, with love, with hatred: it does not matter which." In addition Virginia's need for Vanessa must have made her feel loved and needed. For Virginia the interplay supplied intense, although painful contact with a mother substitute, with hope always held out that this time her sister would come through.

Underlying the limitations of the sisters' relationship was their failure to establish adequate ego identity, the ability to say "This is who I am, this is who I was, this is what I feel and know and think." Bernard, Virginia's alter ego in *The Waves,* beautifully describes this psychological state when he says (1931, pp. 287–288): "But how describe the world seen without a self? There are no words . . . And now I ask 'Who am I?' I have been talking of Bernard, Neville, Jinny, Susan, Rhoda and Louis. Am I all of them? Am I one and distinct? I do not know . . . There is no division between me and them.''

One's identity is formed in that process of separation-individuation in which the toddler gradually differentiates himself or herself from mother and learns to think "This is mother, this is me." Neither Virginia nor Vanessa individuated enough from their mother to enable them to develop a strong sense of who they were. Nor could they help themselves in this respect by identification with their mother, the woman who had lost herself in love. Individuals unsure of their identity are afraid to love a fully available person, because of their fear of losing what fragile sense of self remains. "I will not let myself be attached to one person only," Jinny says (1931, p. 55). "I do not want to be fixed, to be pinioned." A sadomasochistic relationship is a halfway measure that puts distance between two individuals who are involved with each other (Bond, 1981, pp. 376–378). One cannot be engulfed by a person who is only partly there. The relationship of the Stephens sisters was a partial substitute for the wholehearted love relationship both yearned for, but which neither was able to withstand.

Virginia's ambivalence toward her sister is aptly expressed by Jinny in *The Waves* (1931, p. 138), who says, "Our hatred is almost indistinguishable from our love." Rhoda (pp. 293–294) further elaborates on the "mixed blessing" of such relationships when she says: "It is strange that we who are capable of so much suffering, should inflict so much suffering . . . But wait . . . Now that I have reviled you for the blow that sent me staggering among peelings and crumblings and old scraps of meat, I will record how also under your gaze . . . I begin to perceive this, that and the other . . . I regain the sense of the complexity and the reality and the struggle, for which I thank you. And with some pity, some envy and much good will, take your hand and bid you good night."

Did Vanessa's relationship with Virginia contribute to the development of and precipitation of further episodes of her psychosis? I think not. Rather, as previously suggested, the relationship was an attempt on Virginia's part to cure the deficits left by the relationship with her mother, a cure that was a partial success for much of Virginia's life, but that failed at precisely those strategic moments when it was most needed to maintain her precarious emotional health. Vanessa was only a very little girl when

Virginia first called on her to fill the gaps left in her development. Vanessa had problems aplenty of her own. Like a drowning person called on to rescue another floundering swimmer, she had to save her own life first. Virginia asked too much of her. Vanessa was not big enough to answer the call, either in early childhood or when the illness that preceded Virginia's death threatened to overtake her.

VANESSA'S CONTRIBUTION TO VIRGINIA'S GENIUS

Despite the underlying love of the sisters for each other, Vanessa's contribution to the blossoming of Virginia's genius was rather a negative one. Much of the time, in Virginia's adolescence and early adulthood, Vanessa served as enough of a mother substitute to enable Virginia to function, and as such was infinitely more benign than no mother figure at all. But, by and large, the sadomasochistic relationship with Vanessa exacted a tremendous toll on Virginia in the amount of energy that was required to extract the reassurance and expressions of love she required from her sister in order to stay well. As a result, so long as Vanessa was central to Virginia's emotional life, not enough of her strength remained to permit the full flowering of her talents in early adulthood.

Virginia's creative life took a great leap forward with her marriage. Despite a severe breakdown which lasted for over two of the three first years of marriage, she received enough security and support in her relationship with Leonard to enable them to publish three important novels in the first decade of the marriage: *The Voyage Out* (1915), *Night and Day* (1919), and *Jacob's Room* (1922). Although Leonard's support was instrumental in helping Virginia on her creative path, she did not find his love inspirational. Her early books were but a harbinger of the greatness Woolf eventually would achieve.

It was the fulfillment she experienced in her love for Vita that sparked the most creative period of Virginia's life, and inspired the writing of her greatest works: *Mrs. Dalloway* (1925), *To the Lighthouse* (1927), *A Room of One's Own* (1929), and her masterpiece, *The Waves* (1931). Only Vita, of all the loved ones in Virginia's life, could turn the key to the enchanted physical paradise shared with her mother as an infant. As a result, Virginia was able to tap once more the "base upon which life stands," which fed the fountain of inspiration out of which her genius flowed. Vanessa could not serve this function even though Virginia loved her "almost to the point of thought-incest" (1977, p. xvii). For Vanessa was but the sister who was too small to fill her mother's shoes. It took the sensuality of the love affair with Vita to reopen the long-shut portals of ecstasy which supplied the battery, the motor power that fueled the greatest works of Virginia Woolf.

SUMMARY

When little Virginia Stephen turned away from her mother at the rapprochement stage of separation-individuation, she looked to her sister Vanessa for maternal nurturance. But Vanessa, unfortunately, was jealous of the little sister, whose intelligence and beauty was much admired by the adults in the family, and who had intruded into the nursery where Vanessa formerly had reigned supreme in her relationship with their brother Thoby. As a result, she was unable or unwilling to give Virginia the unadulterated, loving response she needed. In addition, Vanessa, like Virginia, suffered from a tenuous sense of selfhood, which forced her to reject Virginia or treat her sadistically, when the psychological need for her sister was the greatest.

A dream of Virginia's suggests that disappointment with her mother led Virginia to transfer her affections to Vanessa, in an attempt to find comfort as well as to get revenge on Mrs. Stephen. The attempt at a "cure" failed, however, as Virginia was made to feel as "much in the way" with her sister as she formerly had felt with her mother.

Because the sisters really were afraid of losing themselves in symbiosis, they reached a sadomasochistic compromise formation in their relationship which partially satisfied the needs of both without threatening the autonomy of either. For example, Virginia would insist on some demonstration of love and affection from Vanessa, who would refuse to give what was demanded of her; Virginia would then nag Vanessa until she reluctantly gave in to the pleas of her sister with some minimal demonstration of affection. As a result, both sisters experienced an intense love-hate relationship which filled the emptiness left by insufficient mothering, without experiencing a loss of self.

The relationship contributed enough to Virginia's stability to enable her to function between her episodes of illness. But the amount of energy expended in the continuous quest for Vanessa's affections surely must have depleted Virginia's limited reserves; a fervor she might better have utilized in the service of her genius.

5

Vita and Virginia
The Reality Behind the Masks

The unwritten story of the Woolf-Sackville romance, in my opinion, is that Vita was the love of Virginia's life. Whereas Vita had many loves besides Virginia, Vita, the rampant "sapphist," in reality was unable to love. In effect, she seduced Virginia, who lived a life as insulated, passive, and protected as "a weevil in a biscuit" (Woolf, 1982, p. 11). Just as Virginia was "all accelerator and no brakes" aggressively, she was all brakes and no accelerator sexually. I believe this psychic deficiency was caused by the early split in her relationship with her mother, which made Virginia's innate sensuality consciously unavailable. Therefore she was dependent upon Vita to initiate the sexual aspects of the relationship. Once sexuality became conscious, it was probably far more enjoyable for Virginia than her biographers have been willing to admit. Vita, unable to remain faithful to anyone, strayed from the relationship after only three or four months. Virginia was heartbroken, and reacted with a minor breakdown. Because of her reluctance to initiate a sexual relationship, she was unable to find a substitute for Vita and thus remained in sexual bondage for the rest of her life.

The relationship with an unfaithful woman duplicated Virginia's early experiences with her mother, who, as we have seen, replaced Virginia at eighteen months with her baby brother, Adrian. Each defection of Vita brought about in Virginia the devastation originally experienced when she first sensed that her mother was lost to her forever. Thus, when told that Vita was going abroad three or four months after the beginning of their sexual relationship, Virginia felt that Vita "was doomed to go to Persia," Virginia's way of experiencing Vita's flight. This tells us that the blind force in living beings which tends to reenact earlier experiences, the repetition compulsion (Freud, 1923, pp. 37–41), was silently at work and that the natural ending of the script had been written long before the beginning of the love affair with Vita. The relationship also duplicated certain aspects of Virginia's relationship with her sister Vanessa, in the sense that Virginia was always the one who pleaded for love, while both Vanessa and Vita resisted her demands.

However, there were therapeutic aspects of Virginia's relationship with Vita. Virginia was able to accomplish with Vita what she could not do with her unavailable mother; again and again Virginia's marvelous gifts enabled her to win back the lover she'd lost, just as the child normally learns he can lose and regain his mother. Thus Virginia's relationship with Vita turned out to be a maturational one. For Virginia, as with the healthy child, each recovery of the beloved woman built yet another block in the edifice of object constancy.

Vita instigated the flowering of Virginia's growth and creativity. By reenacting the ecstatic and frustrating love story with her mother, as well as the sadomasochistic relationship between Virginia and Vanessa, Vita was the catalyst who enabled Virginia to resume her emotional development. Unwittingly, Vita contributed to the maintenance of Virginia's health and sanity for over eighteen years. In addition she served as the primary source of inspiration and creativity for Woolf's most important works, *To the Lighthouse, The Waves,* and *Orlando,* "the most beautiful love letter in history." Just as Leonard was the mainstay that upheld and supported the artist, Virginia Woolf, Vita sparked the motor power that propelled the work of the artist. Virginia was dependent on both to keep lit the lamp of her creativity. When the love affair with Vita finally ended, the light of Virginia's genius dimmed.

The Stage Is Set

By the time she and Vita met in 1922, Virginia Woolf was forty years old and in the full bloom of her professional and marital maturity. She had written three novels and been married for ten years. She also had had three major emotional breakdowns. So far as we know, Vita was the first important woman to appear on the scene after Virginia's marriage.

For two years preceeding their meeting, Virginia had been ill with undiagnosed fever and depression. In searching out the emotional climate that readied her for the romance of her life, several facts stand out. First of all, two years of "undiagnosed fever and depression" fairly scream that something was awry in the personal life of Virginia Woolf. The primary evidence seems to point to the emotional unavailability of Leonard, who was immersed in politics at this time. During this period, minor plaints pepper the diary. For example, the writes (1978, p. 50), "Back from Rodmell, which was disappointing, as if held to our lips the cup of pleasure was dashed from them." Her comment (1978, p. 170–171), "I am suspended between life and death in an unfamiliar way," suggests that this time there was something different about Leonard's absences. Shortly thereafter (p. 173), Virginia wrote, "How can anyone be such a fool as to believe in anyone?"

About this time there appeared persistent underground rumblings about Leonard. He apparently was busier than ever, having been asked to stand for Parliament, and adopted as the Labour Party candidate of the Combined Universities (1978, p. 101). His unavailability upset Virginia greatly. It also raises the question of why Leonard, who was busy throughout his marital life, was unavailable to Virginia, conceivably for the first time.

In addition to her unhappiness about Leonard, Virginia had become estranged from Vanessa. She missed her sister, whose absence left an empty space and in all likelihood revived earlier losses of her mother and half sister Stella. Thus Virginia was ready to replace Vanessa.

Along with her dissatisfaction with Leonard and Vanessa, Virginia, like her father before her, was upset about her work. "I'm a failure as a writer," she wrote (1978, p. 106). "I'm out of fashion; old; shant do any better . . . for half an hour I was as depressed as I ever was . . . Duran refused the book ["Monday or Tuesday"] in America . . . What depresses me is that I have ceased to interest people."

In trying to understand her state of mind at the time, it appears likely that the forty-year-old Virginia was at the nadir of a mid-life depression. Many people feel that this time of life brings the last opportunity to seek out happiness. Dissatisfied with her life, her husband, her relationship with Vanessa, and her work, Virginia, too, must have wondered where else she could look for fulfillment. It is interesting to note that in the year she was to meet Vita, Virginia wrote in her diary (1978, p. 171) that the ethical code of Bloomsbury "allows poaching . . . a change of relationship, a middle-aged relationship, offers new experiences," suggesting that at least in her unconscious she was open to the idea of an affair.

By the time of her first meeting with Vita, Virginia was well on her way to recovery. *Jacob's Room* (1922) had come out, and received some fine reviews. An especially good report from her American publisher, Donald Brace, had revived Virginia's spirits. Although she considered it a mixed blessing, Leonard was doing well in his political career. The *New York Times* had commissioned him to write a monthly article, thereby increasing their income. Even though this made Virginia jealous, she was able to write one month before she and Vita met (1978, p. 212): "On the whole, I'm perfectly satisfied, more so, I think, than ever before . . . and am really very busy, and very happy, and only want to say Time, stand still here."

But before turning the spotlight onto the relationship of Virginia and Vita, it behooves us to look into the character and psychohistory of this woman, this femme fatale Victoria Sackville-West, who was to prove of such major importance in the stability and creativity of Virginia Woolf, and investigate the strains and eddies of Vita's psyche that enabled her to be the instrument of development and disillusion, of passion and despair.

THE OVERTURE

They met at the dinner table of Clive Bell, Virginia's brother-in-law, on December 14, 1922. Vita made no comment in her diary about the meeting. As with her relationship with her sister, Mrs.

Woolf apparently was more intrigued with Vita than Vita was with her, for she wrote in her diary (1978, p. 216): "I am too muzzy-headed to make out anything. This is partly the result of dining to meet the lovely gifted aristocratic Sackville-West last night at Clive's. . . . [she] makes me feel virgin, shy, schoolgirlish."

A few days after she dined with Vita at her house on Ebury Street together with Clive and Desmond McCarthy, Virginia took the initiative into her own hands (Bond, 1967), as she previously had with Vanessa. On December 28, she wrote Vita that the promised copy of *Knole* had never arrived, and complimented her on her poetry. After receiving the book on January 13, she wrote Vita again to comment on "the magnificence of the book" (which, incidentally, is quite different from Virginia's later assessment that Vita Sackville-West wrote "with a pen of brass"), and to invite her to dinner a few days later. After Vita paid her first visit to Hogarth House, her interest was piqued by Virginia's fascination with her, and she wrote to her husband, "I love Mrs. Woolf with a sick passion." The romance of romances had struck its opening note.

The Marriage of Vita and Harold Nicolson

Vita never was really "in love" with Harold. All their married lives, there were others; for Vita, numerous women whom she passionately desired; for Harold, men with whom he had casual sex. Both Nicolsons changed the cast frequently, but the script remained the same. Yet Vita's quieter love for Harold met with a better fate than her passions for women, for these tumultuous "loves" always "wore out." In her youth, they lasted a few weeks or months; in later years, as long as five to seven years, while her marriage, such as it was, lasted until death (Glendinning, p. 54).

I believe that Vita married in order to present a "normal" face to the world. According to her son Nigel (1973, p. 90), throughout his parents' long engagement Vita continued her love affair with Rosamund, her first love. Nicolson writes: "In love with Rosamund, she was teaching herself, willing herself, to love Harold." A few months before her wedding, when Vita was twenty years old, she wrote in her diary (p. 91): "I can see nothing in the future but boredom and pain. I cannot, I cannot, leave everything for him." A few days later she wrote: "I spoke to Rosamund about H. She is the only person who knows the truth. Tonight I think I can never do it." Perhaps, as Nicolson states (p. 3): "If their marriage is seen as a harbour, their love-affairs were mere ports-of-call." It seems more likely that the marriage served primarily as a harbour of propriety in the ultratraditional world of Victorian morality.

Harold's work as a diplomat took him to foreign lands such as Persia and Germany. At these times of separation nostalgic letters reigned between husband and wife, expressing emotions never communicated verbally which perhaps they wished they were able to feel. Vita's letters were filled with sentiment, such as "My darling Hadji, how I miss you!" (p. 208), and "There is no one in the world who counts for me but you, and never will be. I simply can't live without you." This seems a bit difficult to believe, when all she had to do was sail to where he was, be it Berlin or Teheran. And indeed, her son Nigel finds their separations "difficult to explain." According to him (p. 208), the children were well taken care of, and "there was nothing imperative to keep her home." Meanwhile (p. 212), Harold took it for granted that "while he was in Berlin she would stay most of the time at Long Barn, writing her letters of mounting indignation against those who kept him there."

Again, according to Nigel (p. 194), "Vita was always in love. I do not know of any moment in her life when she was not longing to see or hear from the only person who could satisfy that longing." That longing was not for Harold. The pair were chums or buddies and genuinely liked each other, for he was her "best actual playmate" and "merry guide" (p. 33). She needed him as a facade to cover up her deepest inner truths. She needed him to give structure to her life and to protect her from being swept away by her impulsive passionate loves. But she did not love him at the center of her being. As a result she lived a lie, for her primary emotional life lay outside the marriage.

Glendinning (p. 62) gives a revealing account of the first moments after the Nicolson wedding, if Vita's account of it in *Marian Strangeways* is accepted as autobiographical. The husband in the

Knole Castle (two views)

novel wouldn't stand beside his bride in the Great Hall to receive congratulations, but disappeared instead into the library to read a book. If so, it seems that Harold understood the pageantry of the wedding and refused to participate in it. Even more chilling is Vita's "slip" on leaving her home at Knole Castle for their honeymoon. Lavishly dressed in new leopard furs, she started off alone through a back door. The guests hauled her back, saying "You've forgotten something." Vita looked mystified. "Your husband," she was told. Vita's Freudian slip reveals that her wedding was an ostentatious performance staged for the benefit of her mother and society and that Harold was the grandest prop of all.

VITA: THE "AS IF" PERSONALITY

Helene Deutsch (1942) speaks of a type of individual whom she calls an "as if" personality. Such people give the impression of adjusting well, but in truth this effect is based on mimicry and a readiness to adopt whatever reactions may be expected rather than on inner needs. Vita's style of life suggests that she was just such a person. The following passage from a letter to Virginia (DeSalvo & Leaska, 1985, p. 119) bears out this diagnosis: "One ought to have a larger repertoire [of people one cares about]. But there, you see, I am saying 'one ought to,' and that gives away the whole trouble: that I live by theories, or rather they revolve and jostle in my head."

This view of Vita as a false self was corroborated by Virginia in her observation that something inside Vita was "muted." Virginia called it "central transparency." Winnicott (1958, p. 296) named it "the real self," which "exists by not being found" and is protected from discovery by the false self whose function is to keep this true self hidden. Perhaps this was Virginia's major attraction for Vita, that she was not taken in by Vita's false self and insisted she face her innermost feelings.

Vita's as-if persona extended to her relationship with her children as well as her husband. Nigel Nicolson observes (p. 222) that there had always been a gap between his mother and her sons. They had very little in common, and although she wrote regularly (as a good mother should), her letters were constrained as if "her pen needed pushing." He adds, "She was guiltily conscious that she never managed to establish an intimacy with her sons, and thought herself a failure as a mother. . ." Interesting in this light was my observation when visiting the Nicolson home at Sissinghurst Castle. The Nicolson sons had erected a gazebo as a memorial to their father on his death. No comparable memorial commemorated the death of their mother.

Insofar as her husband was concerned, Vita took no interest whatever in his career. According to her son (p. 143), she had a profound ignorance of foreign policy, and "made no effort to acquire even a headline-reader's familiarity with the crises that absorbed Harold's every working day." They would never discuss such things on his return home. It is difficult to understand how a woman supposed to love her husband deeply could fail to take even a minimal interest in the events of his day. In a letter to Virginia (p. 18), Vita stated that as a rule her husband did not

Sissinghurst

The garden at Sissinghurst

allow her to see him when he was depressed. Again, how superficial a marriage that has no room for the husband's feelings of
sadness and depression! This arrangement suited Harold well because he, too, was play-acting at marriage, as suggested by his
letter to Vita (Glendinning, 1983, p. 94): "Oh darling, yesterday
I wanted to kiss you *as if* I loved you, and you turned
aside."[Emphasis mine.]

Glendinning informs us (p. 37) that Vita, too, did not confide
in Harold about important matters in her own life. In fact, many
years into their "happy marriage," when Vita, her woman lover
Edie Lamont, and Harold were on a boat trip together, Vita suffered the hemorrhage requiring a hysterectomy which revealed
advanced cancer. Yet Harold was told nothing about it. Instead,
Vita confided in Edie, the lover she had taken along on their trip.
Furthering the "as-if" hypothesis, Glendinning states (p. 403) that
after injections by the ship's doctor, Vita was well enough to write

The garden at Sissinghurst (another view)

The gazebo—the Nicolson sons' tribute to their father

The plaque at the foot of the tower

Vita's tower room as it is today

deceptively normal letters to friends in England about famous men on board. Most revealing of all is the philosophy expressed by the eighteen-year-old Vita in her novel *Behind the Mask* (1910): In it, the heroine, thrown by her worldly mother into the "matrimonial fishpond," marries a dull devoted Frenchman whom she does not love. "Everyone conceals his or her true feelings behind a mask," Vita wrote. "Is there anyone without the mask? Not the mother, not the wife, not the son." In the book the married heroine does not give up her paramour, but forces each lover to accept her feelings for the other, thus facing up to the reality behind the mask. The novel proves to be prophetic of the Nicolson marriage in which each partner continually was forced to accept the presence of others. In this sense, at least, Vita was "real." That her false self was apparent to others besides Virginia is made clear by Lady Sackville's description of her daughter at age thirty (Glendinning, 1983, p. 123): "She is a difficult person to know. To me, who knows her pretty well, she is a beautiful mask!"

HER PARENTS

In discussing her affair with Rosamund during the months of her engagement, Vita declared, "I seem to be incapable of fidelity" (Glendinning, 1983, p. 51). Vita had a surplus of models for this sexual pattern. Her father, Lord Sackville, first dallied with the young Lady Camden, then had the "stringy wispy Lady Constance" as his paramour. When he got tired of her, he brought in Olive Rubens and her husband to live at Knole Castle.

For years, Lady Sackville tolerated her husband's affairs and his sullenness. Then she gradually began to form her own circle of prominent and wealthy men. First there was "Seery," Lady Sackville's omnipresent obese gentleman companion, who seemed a more consistent presence during Vita's growing-up years than her "Dada." After Seery died, leaving Lady Sackville a fortune, she cultivated a string of millionaires and lonely elderly artists, who included William Waldorf Astor, J. Pierpont Morgan, Auguste Rodin, and Rudyard Kipling.

Lady Sackville shared her marital philosophy with Vita, referring in her diary to frank conversations about the subject. "When I myself married," Lady Sackville wrote (p. 140), "my father cautioned me that the physical side of marriage could not be expected to last more than a year or two, and once, in a broadcast, he said Being 'in love' lasts but a short time—from 3 weeks to 3 years. It has little or nothing to do with the felicity of marriage." The Sackville philosophy proved to be prophetic for Vita as well as her mother, or perhaps was accepted as permission to do as they pleased in their marriages. This may have worked for the Sackvilles; but, in my view, Vita's infidelity contributed significantly to the death of Virginia Woolf.

THE SACKVILLES: MOTHER AND DAUGHTER

In Vita's third novel, *Grey Wethers,* Clare is married to an overindulged, articulate, nonmasculine man, but is in love with a lean, dark, red-shirted gypsy type. Clare "was frightened that a day might come when she would be forced to be true to herself again; when the decent, ordinary, conventional false self should be suddenly abolished" (Glendinning, p. 131). At this period of her life, Vita, like Clare, had given up her lover, Violet Trefusis, and her homosexuality was dormant. But Clare's fear predicted that the day would come when Vita's true self, like Clare's, would burst its bonds and explode into the passionate affair with Violet that nearly destroyed two marriages.

Vita was deprived of her mother's love unless she pretended to be the child her mother wanted instead of the "ugly, sloppy child" her mother said she was. Vita's true self was hidden behind mother and daughter "masks." "Mother used to hurt my feelings and say she couldn't bear to look at me because I was so ugly," wrote Vita in her autobiography (Nicolson, p. 10), "and I used to see myself, plain, lean, dark, unsociable, unattractive—horribly unattractive—rough, and secret."

One day when Vita was ill and very miserable (p. 36), her mother "did her duty" by her child and came to her room once or twice a day holding a little bottle of disinfectant to her nose, and saying that there were three hundred steps between her room and Vita's, and it was a great bore to feel she had to go visit an ill person who was waiting for her. After this dutiful visit was over, Vita would sob with loneliness and sadness. Years later, when she fell ill on her trip to Persia, Vita was to reexperience the feelings of that sick lonely child. "At Karachi with diphtheria," she wrote (*Letters,* p. 21), "and left there alone—I am all alone, and there is no one on this ship who cares whether I live or die."

A revealing anecdote is related by Glendinning (p. 15). It seems that Vita at age eight had embroidered an atrocious yellow and mauve footstool cover for her mother's birthday. This "hideous but loving piece of work" inspired an unpublished sketch of Vita's called *The Birthday,* in which "a wealthy woman of taste subtly rejects the ugly antimacassar her little daughter has so proudly made for her and hurts the child—who has ugly straight hair—to the quick."

Perhaps the most illuminating statement made by Vita about her relationship with her mother (p. 20) is: "She loved me when I was a baby, but I don't think she cared for me as a child, nor do I blame her." Only as an infant was Vita's true self deemed lovable by her mother; after that period only conventional pretensions and superficial goodness were acceptable. As a result, Vita searched all her life in other women for the early mother who had loved her.

It appears that Lady Sackville was no better a mother to the adult Vita than she was to the child. For example, she did not attend the wedding of her only child at Knole Castle, as she was unable "to bear the strain of parting." Other people put it less kindly and gossiped that she certainly would have attended "if she had been the center of attention." After her marriage, Vita became increasingly disillusioned with her mother. When, characteristically, Lady Sackville behaved badly at the birth of Vita's first son, Benedict, she wrote her mother (Glendinning, p. 74): "I know now you don't love me, and that at the very first strain put upon your love you are ready to fling me aside like an old glove . . . you have given me your lavish generosity, it is true, but the generosity of the heart which I should have valued infinitely more you have denied me."

Because her mother could not love the child Vita as she was, roughness, naughtiness, and all, she was sentenced all her life to hide behind her false self with her "central transparency" forever obscured, in the unyielding search for unconditional love. Vita put this creed in words to Harold (p. 188): "To love me whatever I do." Virginia Wolf came closest to meeting this need, had Vita only been able to accept it.

LADY SACKVILLE THE TEASE

In examining Vita's character and personality, it seems clear that Lady Sackville was far more influential than Lord Sackville in their daughter's development, and that Vita was much more like her mother than her father. After visiting the Sackville ancestral home, Knole, Woolf wrote (1980, p. 125) that the aristocratic lineage, which "had gone on for hundreds of years . . . was not remarkable . . . no particular awe or any great sense of difference or distinction. They are not a brilliant race." Lady Sackville, on the other hand, when only a teenager, was a brilliant hostess to her father, who was an ambassador to Washington. Daughter also of an obscure Spanish dancer, this woman of boundless vitality and magnetic charm made a brilliant match with Lord Sackville, one of the most eligible scions of Britain, and as previously noted, was successful in attracting many distinguished suitors. Scores of people adored her (she kept a list of her 25 marriage proposals) and, according to Glendinning (p. 145), "It was an adoration that she subconsciously exacted." Vita seems to have inherited her mother's vitality and charm, and to have identified with and emulated her success at seduction.

One of Lady Sackville's former amoretti wrote her (p. 61): "I tell you, you are charming, fascinating, heaven knows what. There is no end to your perfections . . . You are an accomplished mistress in love. You play with it and use it and manage it, like a seagull the wind, on which he floats but is never carried away." Her son Nigel adds: "She loved power . . . She could be cruel . . . She was both tender and fierce. . ." In baser terms, Lady Sackville was a tease who promised more than she delivered. Rodin, deeply in love with her, was permitted "liberties but not license." Poor Seery was given an even harder time. According to Vita (p. 21), "She bullied and charmed him, fought with him, bewitched him, until he simply could not exist without her. . ." Lady

Sackville used to tell Vita that Seery was in love with her and came whenever possible to importune her at her bedroom door. She arranged with her daughter that in case Seery fell into a fit outside her bedroom, Vita should come and wake her mother, and together they would bump him downstairs to his own bedroom, and that by slipping him down from step to step they could manage to shift his enormous mass without awakening anyone.

According to Glendinning (p. 16): "Victoria enslaved her daughter as she enslaved others," overindulging her with material objects and smothering her with love when she felt like it, ignoring and condemning her as ugly when it suited her. As a result, Vita wrote, "She wounded and dazzled and fascinated and charmed me by turns . . . if ever the phrase 'turn one's heart to water' meant anything, it meant when my mother looked at you and smiled . . . No wonder I loved and wondered; no wonder my father loved and got hurt; He got hurt beyond healing, and then he began to hurt his wife in return." Surely Vita was talking about her own patterns in love as well as her mother's. Lady Sackville hurt her daughter "beyond healing"; and in an attempt to master the pain, Vita, like her father, began to hurt others in return. Leaska states (DeSalvo & Leaska, 1985, p. 13) that Vita "seemed forever fanning the embers of love and was forever stepping back from its blaze." Several of her ex-lovers (Geoffrey Scott, Hilda Mattheson) died within a few years of being rejected by Vita. Christopher St. John on her death left behind an excruciating indictment of her relationship with Vita, who called the love journal "Christopher's horrifying document . . . the shattering record of her friendship with me." Vita, late in her life, apparently became aware of how much and how often she had hurt Harold. "I have treated him badly enough in the past and must make it up to him now," she wrote.

VITA THE LOVER

In her autobiography (Nicolson, 1973, p. 11), Vita acknowledges that in her childhood she was cruel to other children, and gives the following example (Glendinning, 1983, p. 14): "There were 5 of them, 4 girls and a boy. The boy and I were allies; the

4 girls were our victims. The boy and I made a practice of tying the 4 girls up to trees and of thrashing their legs with nettles. Also we stuffed their nostrils with putty, and gagged their mouths with handkerchiefs. No real hostility was implied," Vita wrote later, with only partial insight. "The girls enjoyed it masochistically, as much as the boy and I, sadistically."

When we consider Vanessa's early sadistic glee which caused Virginia to "turn a lovely flaming red" (Bell, Vol. 1, 1972, p. 24), it is clear that her interaction with Vanessa was a paradigm for that which was to follow with Vita. For the two women were programmed for each other by similar sadomasochistic experiences in childhood.

In adulthood, Vita's cruelty, like Lady Sackville's, consciously extended to her lovers. Speaking of her romance with Violet Trefusis, probably the most passionate love affair of her life, Vita (Glendinning, 1983, p. 27), with a notable absence of guilt, describes how she treated her lover "with unvarying scorn, my one piece of really able handling, which kept her tied to me as no proof of devotion would have kept her." Glendinning observes (p. 50) that, at twenty, Vita was already displaying "the capacity for sustaining multiple relationships," and the "disinclination to let anyone who loved her go—keeping them on a string, rebuffing them if they asked too much of her, but drawing in the line sharply if they showed signs of straying."

When her first lover, Rosamund, wrote that she was enjoying a romance with a naval instructor, Vita, who herself was besieged with swains, "took instantaneous revenge in a stinging letter designed to hurt Rosamund as much as possible" (Glendinning, 1983, p. 55). Vita was sarcastic and cold, "saying she had decided to take Violet to . . . Florence and that she was afraid she would not have time to write." As previously noted, Harold was also a major recipient of Vita's sadism. Three weeks after the birth of their first child, Harold was spending weekday nights in London. According to a letter quoted by Glendinning (p. 73), he wrote: "How I long to see my darling—and be soundly snubbed when I come in—like you used to do at Cple . . . You used to go on writing with your pretty little head over your table and refusing to turn around." His letter two days later was of similar tone; "Oh my darling please don't snub me tomorrow. Vita I simply worship you, my own saint." It seems Vita's sadistic techniques worked as well with Harold as with her female lovers. He was cheered up, however, by a visit from his male lover, Pierre Lacretelle, while Rosamund joined Vita at Knole.

Thus by following Lady Sackville's blueprint for love, Vita's list of known lovers grew to read like her mother's—Rosamund, Violet, Geoffrey Scott, Margaret Voight, Harold, Mary Campbell, Hilda Matheson, Evelyn Irons, Dorothy Wellesley, Gwen St. Aubyn, and, the biggest coup of all, the virginal Virginia Woolf.

Virginia, with her background of a sadomasochistic love relationship with Vanessa, was easily ensnared by Vita's magnetic sadism. According to DeSalvo and Leaska (1985, p. 13), "Vita's emotional terrain . . . contained a dark sadistic province" that Virginia seems to have felt and accepted from the beginning, and which prepared her to take on the submissive role in their relationship. Little phrases scattered throughout the letters indicate that in contrast to the relative lack of awareness in the relationship with her sister, Virginia experienced a conscious pleasure in the small abuses Vita caused her to suffer. That Virginia was conscious of Vita's sadism is evident in her question, "Is it true you love giving pain?" In one of their earlier letters Virginia recognized her own masochistic contribution to the relationship. "I enjoyed your intimate letter. . ." she wrote. "It gave a great deal of pain . . . which is no doubt the first stage of intimacy . . . Never mind: I enjoyed your abuse very much." Vita responded in kind on January 11, 1926 (1977, p. 85), when she wrote: "I find life altogether intoxicating—its pain no less than its pleasure,—in which Virginia plays no mean part."

On February 9, 1927, Vita wrote Virginia from Teheran, "I suppose it is good for the soul to be hurt and perplexed perpetually. I know at least that I miss you damnably; and would rather be hurt by that, and have something to hold on to than flounder in a quicksand that never bruises but only smothers" (Bond, 1981). And on February 18, 1927, Virginia wrote, "Sweet Honey: . . . Yes, I want you more and more. You'll like to think of me as unhappy I know. Well, you can. . ."

DeSalvo and Leaka make the penetrating observation (1985, pp. 14–15) that by the time Virginia wrote *Orlando,* the protagonist could only have made his first entrance committing an act of violence—"slicing at the head of a moor." In one of her novels, Vita has her hero say to his lover, "I should like to chain you up . . . naked and beat you and beat you until you screamed." "Everybody always betrayed one sooner or later, and usually gave one away to someone else," she wrote Virginia. "What one wanted was always destroyed." "Something always does, when one wants a thing too passionately" (DeSalvo & Leaska, 1985, pp. 20–21). To captivate and keep one's victim chained up in a state of longing, to whet the victim's appetite just enough to keep the quarry "on a string" forever; such behavior would ensure that Vita need never again experience the pains of helpless longing, and assured the beloved's availability should the need arise. For this is what Vita learned at her mother's knee, how to turn the tables against the oppressor and at the same time get revenge against mother. This is what Vita did to all her loves. And this is what she did to Virginia Woolf.

THE ROMANCE

It did not take long for the "fun and games" to begin. Vita invited Virginia to be a member of the famous PEN club. Virginia refused. Vita, feeling snubbed, cooled off for the remainder of 1923 and early 1924, falling passionately but temporarily in love with Geoffrey Scott. Early in 1924, Virginia invited Vita to contribute a book to the Hogarth Press, and Vita responded by writing *Seducers in Ecuador*. Then, soon after Virginia visited Long Barn and Knole, the relationship between the women began in earnest with a jab in a letter from Virginia to Vita that "You write letters of impersonal frigidity." Vita responded with a counterpunch: "I believe you look upon everything, human relations included [as copy]. Oh, yes, you like people through the brain better than through the heart." Virginia answered with the previously quoted letter admitting her enjoyment of Vita's abuse. Vita followed up with ". . . what on earth in my letter could have given you a great deal of pain . . . Do you ever mean what you say, or say what you mean? or do you just enjoy baffling the people who try to creep a little nearer?"

During the following year the two women met infrequently

in London. As Vita freed herself from her lover, Geoffrey Scott, she and Virginia became increasingly close. The climax between Vita Sackville-West and Virginia Woolf was about to occur. On October 11, 1925, the "fun and games" began in earnest, as Vita dropped the first of a long series of bombs. Although she had remained at home many times when her husband was sent abroad, Vita announced to Virginia that Harold had been posted by the Foreign Office to the British Legation in Teheran and that she was accompanying him. Virginia responded with the despairing innocence that prompted the following letter: "My dear Vita: But for how long? Forever? I am filled with envy and despair. Think of seeing Persia—think of never seeing you again. The doctor has sent me to bed; all writing forbidden. So this is my swan song. But come and see me."

From now on, for the rest of her life, I believe that many of Virginia Woolf's moods were to be tied to her relationship with Vita, whose usual strategy was to bring immediate results. Virginia first responded in typical fashion, by becoming ill. But this time it did not last for long. For on December 17 she went to stay with Vita at Long Barn (Harold was already in Teheran), when they became lovers for the first time. As a result her illness was temporarily "cured." Vita's "defection" was to have profound results for Virginia on a professional as well as personal basis, for shortly after, Vita left for Teheran. Virginia (as noted in Chapter 2) followed her father's example of sublimating his sorrow in creativity. She began *To the Lighthouse* and, by February, was writing "massively." In so doing she helped herself to master the pain of Vita's absence, as well as the traumas suffered years before at the deaths of her mother and half sister Stella.

In May, when Vita returned, the two saw each other frequently. But Vita had ensured that the affair would self-destruct, and sought out her typical cure; she began another affair, this time with Dorothy Wellesley, to whom she dedicated her prize-winning poem, *The Land,* and of whom she saw more than she did Virginia. On July 21, Virginia suffered "a whole nervous breakdown" in miniature. Six weeks later, Vita and Dorothy traveled together to Normandy, and Virginia's suffering intensified, along with the symptoms of an impending breakdown. On September 15, she wrote in her diary (1978, p. 110), "Oh its beginning its coming—the horror—physically like a painful wave swelling about the heart—tossing me up.'' On September 28, she noted: ''Intense depression: I have to confess that this has overcome me several times since September 6 [the date Vita and Dorothy went away to Normandy].''

On October 3, Vita wrote (p. 123): ''I feel I have been very tiresome, what with saying I would come and not coming, and one thing and another. But if you knew how uncertain everything has been. . .'' But it is clear that Virginia was not reassured. When her moods were at their lowest point, Virginia was unable to write even in her diary; there were no entries until October 30.

She did write Vita two letters during this period. however; letters which remained unanswered. On September 15, while reading Vita's *Passage to Teheran,* Virginia noted, ''How I should like to know this woman,'' and then thought ''I do.'' This reaction, along with the lack of diary entries, indicates that Virginia had become estranged from her feelings, and that the pain, anxiety, and rage she experienced were so unbearable that she had to banish them from consciousness. But the warded-off pain is expressed somatically—Virginia has headaches and a pain in her back.

On November 19, in a letter to Vita, Woolf expresses her fear that Vita will tire of her ''one of these days'' as she is ''so much older,'' and therefore she, Virginia, has ''to take her little precautions. That's why I put the emphasis on recording rather than feeling.'' Then follows the famous passage (1977, p. 302) in which she brilliantly turns the tables on Vita by pinpointing her alienation and unyielding heart of stone: ''And isn't there something obscure in you? There is something that doesn't vibrate in you; It may be purposely—you don't let it: but I see it with other people, as well as with me: something reserved, muted—God knows what. . . . It's in your writing too, bye the bye. The thing I call central transparency—something fails you there, too.'' Out of her pain and grief, Virginia understood why their relationship was failing, and why Vita's mother had called her ''a beautiful mask.''

But Virginia had shot the one bullet that still worked with Vita, she had seen through the ''as if'' nature of Vita's defenses and had recognized that Vita was not a ''real'' person. ''Damn the woman,'' Vita wrote her husband, ''she has put her finger on it. There is something muted . . . Something that doesn't vibrate, something that doesn't come alive . . . It makes everything I do [i.e., write] a little unreal; gives the effect of having been done from the outside. It is the thing that spoils me as a writer . . . It is what spoils my human relationships, too, but that I mind less." As a result of her perceptiveness, Virginia temporarily won the power struggle with Vita and revived her respect. The next day the Nicolsons invited the Woolfs to the ballet, and Virginia wrote in her diary (November 21), "So we go on—a spirited, creditable affair, I think, innocent (spiritually) and all gain."

A few days later, when Vita received a copy of Virginia's latest book, *Mrs. Dalloway* (1925), she fell even more in love with the genius Virginia, the writer that Vita wished she could be. For narcissistic people, according to Freud (1914), can love only wished-for aspects of *themselves,* what one is, was, or (as in the case of Vita), what one would like to be. "I wish," she declared in renewed adoration (DeSalvo & Leaska, 1985, p. 151), ". . . we could put the clock back a year [to the time they first made love]. I should like to startle you again—even though I didn't know then that you were startled." Virginia Woolf, because of her insight and fame as a writer, had won the first round with Vita; but there were to be many more rounds in the future and Virginia was not always to be so "lucky."

Virginia Matures

Now that Vita had fallen madly in love with Virginia again, the women experienced a brief "second honeymoon." "Dearest Vita (Now why did I say that?)," Virginia wrote breathlessly on December 8, 1926. "Yes, Monday . . . Please come and bathe me in serenity again. Yes, I am wholly and entirely happy" (1977, p. 306).

The brief period of ecstasy apparently was more than Vita could tolerate, for on January 28 she left again for Persia. This time she was flanked by another lover, Dorothy Wellesley, and Leigh Ashton, a friend. According to DeSalvo and Leaska (p. 163), Virginia's grief at Vita's departure was not quite so acute as it had been the year before. For it seems that Virginia was learning that, unlike her mother, who disappeared forever, Vita's absence was temporary. In contrast to the infant who often dies without a mother, Virginia found that although she had bouts of depression she could survive four months without Vita.

In fact a few days later she wrote Vita: "I could think only of you as being very distant and beautiful and calm—a lighthouse in clear waters . . . I feel dissipated and aimless for some reason . . . Then it's you being away—I am at the mercy of people, of moods, feel lonely, like something pitiable which can't make its wants known. How you have demoralized me." The first indication of her emotional growth in the relationship had made itself felt. Unlike the previous year, Virginia could now experience grief without her usual freezing. This time she was able to feel her pain acutely. "It gets worse steadily—your being away," she wrote Vita on February 5. "I'm settling down to wanting you, doggedly, dismally, faithfully—I hope that pleases you. It's damned unpleasant for me, I can assure you. I had a sort of idea that I'd cheat the devil, and put my head under my wing, and think of nothing. But it wont work—not at all. I want you this Saturday more than last and so it'll go on."

A letter to Virginia on March 4 indicates that indeed Vita not only knew what Virginia needed from her but yearned to supply it. And to some degree she did. "I have a game which I play all by myself," she wrote. "It consists of finding, and piecing together, the scattered fragments of Virginia's world. You see, this world was once whole and complete, and then one day some inner cataclysm burst it into pieces, like the planet which burst into what is now the asteroids." Vita's diagnosis of Virginia's fragmented personality was correct. Like a psychoanalyst, Vita served as a transference figure, a surrogate-mother image who to some degree was able to help Virginia reintegrate her inner world. But Vita's own need for distance, her lack of constancy and need to reject before being rejected kept her from being the ever-glowing lighthouse about whose radiance Virginia might have reconstructed her personality. As it had been with Vanessa, Virginia's need for Vita largely was a maturational one. She needed Vita in order to pick up her development where her mother had left off. In the light of the overwhelming urge of her growth force (see Chapter 1), Virginia's desperate need for Vita becomes understandable.

That Vita was as vital to Virginia's physical health as for her emotional well-being is evident in the following letter (Woolf, 1978): "It's a great refuge to think I could fly to Long Barn— How you cured me when I was ill before (June 1927)! Potto [Virginia's pet name] would be happy. I shall be in robust health by the time you're back—27 days now."

But Vita, inconstant Vita, returned from Teheran on May 5, and true to her character, fell in love with Mary Campbell, wife of the poet, Roy Campbell. And as before, when Virginia sent a copy of her latest book, *To the Lighthouse,* Vita's love was re-kindled. "The clock seems to have been put back a year. . ." she wrote with passion. "But everything is blurred to a haze by your book . . . and that is the only thing that seems real . . . Darling, it makes me afraid of you. Afraid of your penetration and love-liness and genius. . . . I do really love you more than before, for it. You always said I was a snob, and perhaps that is a form of snobbishness. But I do . . . it makes you more precious, more of an enchanter."

Nevertheless, Vita's affair with Mary continued and, by May 29, Virginia predictably developed "chills and headaches" which landed her in bed as usual. And, as always, when she suspected that Vita was having an affair and was not quite ready to face it, there are no entries in Virginia's diary for several weeks.

Two months later, something different occurred in the relationship, and the state of Virginia's health, which further illustrates the growth Virginia was experiencing. This time, instead of becoming depressed, Virginia got angry, allowing herself an affect previously suppressed with her mother and sister. Vita maliciously wrote, "I like making you jealous, my darling, (and shall continue to do so,) but it's ridiculous that you should be" (DeSalvo & Leaska, 1985, p. 214). Pasted on the reverse side was an illustration of a dolphin, which I believe was a private symbol the women used to represent their lovemaking (and which, incidentally, was originally the term of endearment Virginia called Vanessa), an-notated, "Dolphin (Delphinus delphis) is an agile animal executing amusing gambols." Virginia responded immediately with "Yes you are an agile animal—no doubt about it, but as to your gambols being diverting . . . at 4 o'clock in the morning, I'm not so sure. Bad, wicked beast! . . . You only be a careful dolphin in your gambolling, or you'll find Virginia's soft crevices lined with hooks."

Virginia's jealousy, however, continued unabated, as Vita's affair with Dorothy Wellesley flourished. "Dear Mrs. N," Virginia wrote on September 2, "I won't belong to the two of you, or to the one of you, if the two of us belong to the one. In short, if Dottie's yours, I'm not." Vita answered, "Don't go right away from me. I depend on you more than you know." Nevertheless, the affair with Dottie prevailed. Virginia wrote on September 21 that she was feeling "rather melancholy." Vita "innocently" answered, "My darling, why melancholy? I thought you were not quite yourself the other day, and wondered if it were all my imagination."

But Virginia's "cure" for her jealousy was to grow out of her newfound strength, as well as her genius. With a profound passion she awoke out of her melancholia and threw herself into *Orlando: A Biography* (1926), a tale that transcended time and space and pain and madness to become "the greatest love letter in history"; a saga of the regal Sackvilles who had danced their way down the centuries, the story of the gallivanting boy-girl Vita, who had bedazzled her way into the bedrooms of so many women. And as she wrote, Virginia knew what it was to be Vita, how to love and re-find one's loved one, and to possess her around the clock. And as she lost and regained Vita, Virginia mastered the loss of her mother and sisters again and again and again.

Although Vita continued her various affairs, Virginia's obsession with *Orlando* cured her depression. A month later, her high spirits continued as she wrote: "I think on the whole this is our happiest autumn. So much work; and success now; and life on easy terms . . . I write so quick I cant get it typed before lunch. This I suppose is the main backbone of my autumn—Orlando." Virginia had found her lighthouse, found it in her art rather than a beloved person. For her newly discovered strength had put her in touch with her rage and given her a new sense of well-being, which gave her the courage to "tell Vita off" as she never had been able to do before. "I made Vita cry the other night; quietly, unselfconsciously," Virginia wrote in her diary (1980, p. 165). " 'I hate being bored'," I said, of her Campbells and Valery Taylors; and this she thought meant I should be tired of her." For the first time, Virginia had turned the tables on Vita from a position of power. As a result, Vita wrote the next day: "I have been so really wretched since last night. I felt suddenly that the whole of my life was a failure, insofar as I seemed incapable of creating one single perfect relationship." Vita continued her affairs, it is true. But, for a while at least, Virginia's moods were independent of Vita's behavior. For the time being, her illness was "cured."

OBJECT CONSTANCY

According to Kaplan (1978, pp. 25–58), when all goes well during the first five months of life, the infant is free to move into the world of enchantment and delight, secure in the knowledge that when he is ready to return, mother will be there. If the child develops naturally, becoming ever more separate and independent, the internal experience of a protective mothering presence develops alongside him. Such a child becomes increasingly able, during the third year of life, to substitute the reliable image of a nurturing mother for her actual presence. This image, which remains stable regardless of internal need or dissatisfaction with those about him, frees the child to develop his relationship with the world and its occupants without psychological impediment.

According to Ray (1988, p. 238), "With the attainment of object constancy, there is no need for compulsive love nor is there need to maintain a persistently hostile attitude . . . There is a capacity for transient symbiotic unity, tolerance for reciprocal dependency, and the capacity to assimilate both admiration and disapproval. While there is pleasure in pleasing others, the attainment of object constancy helps to free the individual from excessive need to please. The capacity to love and to believe one is loved is assured." All of these qualities blossomed in Virginia as her relationship with Vita mellowed. Through her love of Vita, Virginia was able to rediscover and strengthen her "good internal mother." Thus she grew to understand that, whatever the exigencies of her lover's personality, she, Virginia, had the power to preserve within herself an untarnished image of love. Whether they saw each other four times a year or twenty, whether Vita had one lover or ten, Virginia gradually learned to hold on to the feeling that Vita loved her and could always belong to her internally in affection and friendship. And as her security in Vita's affection enabled her to put to rest her mother-longing, Virginia's writing became an act of creation that sustained and held her as it spread over the world, replacing for the time being the more ordinary variety of human love. Nurtured by her love for Vita during the active years of their romance, the great literary masterpieces *To the Lighthouse, Orlando,* and *The Waves* flowed forth from the golden pen of Virginia Woolf.

The end of the love affair with Vita marked the finish of the most creative period of Virginia's life. According to Roda Neugebauer (1986), "The original state of being, this first union, leaves a memory trace, is an analog of experience which throughout life we can return to. It is derivatives of this early way of being, the finding and losing of analogs of this state, which form a core of the creative process." Similarly, the basis for Virginia's creativity was the rich sensuality of the early period of oneness with her mother, which was rekindled by love for Vita. So long as Virginia was in love, the rich milk of creativity poured forth from her. When their love affair cooled, the development of object constancy, that ability to keep Vita alive inside of her, had matured sufficiently to allow Virginia to remain sane and productive. But her work no longer measured up to the quality of her former masterpieces. Although *The Years, Three Guineas,* and *Roger Fry* certainly were well written, Virginia had lost the golden touch characteristic of her writing in the 1920s. Thus Virginia's love for her mother proved to be the bedrock of her creativity as well as "the basis upon which life stands."

THEIR SEX LIVES

Careful study of Virginia Woolf's letters and diaries leaves little doubt that the sexual relationship between Virginia and Vita was a passionate one and continued for many years, although much that has been written about the affair tends to deny this. Quentin Bell, for example, comments (1972, p. 119) that "there may have been—on balance I think that there probably was—some caressing, some bedding together. But . . . I doubt very much whether it was of a kind to excite Virginia or to satisfy Vita.'' Vita herself "reassured" Harold in a letter to him early in her relationship with Virginia (Glendinning, 1926, p. 165) that she had "gone to bed with her (twice), but that's all," for she was "scared to death of arousing physical feelings in her, because of the madness." A careful reading of Virginia's and Vita's diaries and letters, however, uncovers many sexual innuendoes and belies the truth of Bell's belief and Vita's avowals. For example, Moore states (1984, p. 14) that "Quentin Bell's curious picture of a 'sexless Sappho' is hardly consonant with her letter to Violet Dickinson, written in July 1903: 'It is astonishing what depths—hot volcano depths—your finger has stirred in Sparroy'." Virginia herself wrote in *Orlando* (1926, p. 209) that "every secret of a writer's soul, every experience of his life, every quality of his mind is written large in his works." The following quotes, "written large," may reveal Virginia's sexual secrets.

On September 25, 1927, Virginia wrote to Vita: "But I own I'd like to see you . . . It's the last chance of a night before London's chastity begins. . ." Shortly after (October 10, 1927), Vita wrote: "But how right I was . . . to force myself upon you at Richmond [in January 1923], and so lay the train for the explosion which happened on the sofa in my room here when you behaved so disgracefully and acquired me forever." On December 5, 1927, Virginia wrote in tone similar to that which she used with Vanessa (1977, pp. 442–3): "Forget everybody else. Should you say, if I rang you up to ask, that you were fond of me? If I saw you would you kiss me? If I were in bed would you—"

And least ambiguous of all, Virginia wrote to Vita, years after they were supposed to have stopped "bedding down once or twice" (April 5, 1929): ". . . I told Nessa the story of our passion in a chemists shop the other day. But do you really like going to bed with women she said—taking her change. And how do you do it?" A few days later (June 10, 1929) Vita wrote to Virginia: "I shall feel forlorn in London with no Virginia when I go up . . . No bunloaf—no affection—no Potto to stroke. Damn." And again, Vita wrote (July 24, 1929): "I told you I missed Potto and Virginia, those silky creatures with a barb under their fur—and so I do, and wonder whether they will come and stay with me when I get back? . . . Virginia would like her nice big bed and coffee at eleven—and all the affection that would be shown her at hours licit and illicit."

Nevertheless, all was not well with the relationship. Vita was having many serious affairs, with Dorothy Wellesley, Hilda Matheson, and Evelyn Irons. Virginia was upset to the point of headaches, which she stated were due at least in part to a particular deceitfulness on the part of Vita. She had gone on a French holiday with Hilda which she told Virginia was spur-of-the-moment, but Virginia inadvertently found out from her friend Janet Vaughn that the trip had been planned months in advance. If the sexual relationship truly were nonexistent, one must wonder why Vita had to "deceive" Virginia, and why Vita did not have the right to go away with whomever she pleased. Virginia grieved deeply for the loss of Vita. On July 25, 1931, Virginia wrote the following poignant, seemingly humorous letter (1978, p. 362); "Potto is dead. For about a month (you have not been here for a month and I date his decline from your last visit) I have watched him failing. First his coat lost lustre; than he refused biscuits; finally gravy. When I asked him what ailed him he sighed, but made no answer. The other day coming unexpectedly into the room, I found him wiping away a tear. He still maintained unbroken silence. Last night it was clear that the end was coming. I sat with him holding his paw in mine, and felt the pulse grow feebler. At 7:45 he breathed deeply, I leant over him. I just caught and was able to distinguish the following words—"Tell Mrs. Nick that I love her . . . she has forgotten me. But I forgive her and. . . . die . . . of . . . a . . . broken . . . heart!" He then expired, and so shall I very soon." What a "joke"! A lovelorn creature dies of a broken heart. If the letter were a dream the prognosis for the dreamer would be bleak indeed.

By 1933 it was clear that the romantic part of the relationship was permanently over. Vita was seriously involved with her sister-in-law, Gwen St. Aubyn, for years, as well as with others, and no longer was sexually interested in Virginia. The two women saw each other much less than formerly. When they did meet, it was only for an afternoon now and then in the company of Leonard, or Vita's sons or lovers. Virginia's sentiments about this time are brought out in a letter to Vita on September 30, 1933: "Mary [a fantasy] makes love to me—yes: other people dont. I dare say at this very minute you're couched with some herring griller in the straw God damn you. . ."

By 1935 it was obvious, even to Virginia, that Vita was not interested in reviving the romance. On February 15, 1935, she poignantly wrote: "I am longing for an adventure, dearest creature. But would like to stipulate for at least 48 1/2 minutes alone with you. Not to say or do anything in particular. Mere affection— to the memory of the porpoise in the pink window" (1979, p. 370).

On November 15, 1937, Virginia answered a letter in which Vita had addressed her as "My dear and once Virginia" in a manner that makes clear that she is ever ready to resume their former relationship: "Why 'once' Virginia? . . . just because you choose to sit in the mud in Kent and I on the flags of London, that's no reason why love should fade is it? Why the pearls and the porpoise should vanish. . . . Because, my dear Vita, whats the use of saying 'once Virginia' when I'm alive here and now? So's Potto if it comes to that."

But, in my opinion, Virginia's letters and diaries make clear that although she longed for a sexual "rapprochement," Vita's character structure made certain that Virginia was doomed to long in vain. For Vita had been programmed to cut off her love relationships with cruelty, while Virginia was "doomed" by the repetition compulsion to wait for her beloved forever.

THE RIPENING

The outbreak of World War II seemed to mature Vita, and she grew to appreciate Virginia's loyalty and friendship, if not her sexuality. She even gave evidence that she valued Virginia's friendship more than her changing lovers, whom she called "those cheap and easy loves." She stood by Virginia, sympathizing with her greatly on the death of her nephew Julian, and sending her frequent gifts of food from her farm during those years of physical as well as emotional deprivation. Virginia's feeling for Vita became even sturdier at this time, and required ever less affirmation from her former lover. "Let us write to one another sometimes," she wrote Vita on September 16, 1939. "I find that there are few people these days who give me any sense of real contact, but you certainly do" (1980, p. 429).

And on December 3 (1980, p. 429), she wrote to thank Vita for her book, *Country Notes:* "I shall keep it by my bed, and when I wake in the night—no, I shant use it as a soporific but as a sedative: a dose of sanity and sheep dog in this scratching, clawing, and colding universe."

And in one of her last communications to Vita (1980, p. 430), it appears that the internalization process is complete. Virginia wrote on March 12, 1940: "Oh what a pleasure to get your letter! And how odd!—I was saying to L. I felt that you felt we were out of touch: as for myself, I never feel out of touch with Vita . . . And how I long to hear from your own lips what's been worrying you—for you'll never shake me off—no, not for a moment do I feel ever less attached."

Despite the horrors raging both within and all about her, it seems that Virginia Woolf had finally grown up. How tragic, then, that these internal and external exigencies could not permit the enjoyment of her hard-won maturity for very long.

SUMMARY

Virginia Woolf was very ready for the advent of Vita Sackville-West into her life. In December 1922 her diaries note depression and dissatisfaction over Leonard's lack of availability, the increased distancing of her sister Vanessa, a temporary feeling of failure about her work, and what appears to be a severe mid-life crisis. Unresolved psychological difficulties which had caused Virginia to split off sexuality from consciousness, as well as a lifelong sadomasochistic relationship with her sister Vanessa, had left Virginia particularly vulnerable to the exigencies of Vita's character.

Vita had been seduced and abandoned repeatedly by her own mother, whose style of loving Vita adopted in order to master the pain and frustration it caused her. As a result she treated her numerous lovers, including Virginia Woolf, with great psychological cruelty. Vita would promise a whole world of love, deliver it for a brief while, and then sadistically withdraw, giving just enough to keep her victims tied to her forever. This manner of evoking and then frustrating great passion unlocked in Virginia the torrents of love and need which had been split off from consciousness for close to forty years, enabling her to sustain the love, hate, and grief which had been hidden from herself. The experience had great therapeutic effect in a manner reminiscent of a successful psychoanalysis, as the adult Virginia discovered that she was able to master on a conscious level the deluge of affect that her infantile ego had been unable to handle. This attainment led to greater ego strength and ever increasing object constancy.

Vita also reawakened in Virginia the exquisite sensibility she had experienced during the symbiotic phase. As a result, when her longing for mothering temporarily could be put to rest, Virginia was able to dip into this fountain of sensuality as well as her new-found pool of love, hate, and grief, to create the great masterpieces for which she is famous. When the love affair between the women cooled, the caliber of Virginia's work deteriorated. While it remains technically excellent, it no longer reaches the heights of artistry achieved during the period of the passionate romance. Thus it is clear that Vita, in reopening Virginia's storehouse of affect, both inspired her great masterpieces of art and helped overcome the devastating effects of crippling infantile experiences with her mother. Therefore, we can state that Vita Sackville-West was of primary importance in determining the course for Virginia Woolf of both her psychosis and her genius.

6

Virginia Woolf and the Death Instinct

THE PLEASURE PRINCIPLE

According to Freud's theory of the Death Instinct (1923), "The final goal of all organic life . . . must be . . . an ancient starting point, which the living being left long ago, and to which it harks back again by all the circuituous paths of development. . . . The inanimate was there before the animate . . . the goal of all life is death." As Freud conceived of it, life in a sense is a disturber of the timeless rest, which counteracts the pull to nonexistence by instinctual and ego gratifications which differ at each stage of development. We stay alive because of the potentialities for pleasure that existence offers; when those possibilities dwindle, then life itself begins to flicker out. The tasks and satisfactions of growth, of psychosexual development, of successful utilization of energy at each level, blot out the pull toward nonexistence. In catastrophic conditions such as psychosis, trauma, deep mourning, and world tragedy, when most mature forms of gratification are inaccessible, the individual tends to regress to the previous stage of development where earlier forms of satisfaction are available. If fulfillment at that level is not forthcoming, a person will regress to an even earlier stage. This developmental slide will continue until the individual reaches some level, no matter how primitive, where pleasure can be achieved. When that person is no longer held to the course, so to speak, by manifold gratifying possibilities, then the innate tendency in all living matter will impel him toward the earliest condition of peace and quiescence—nonexistence. This principle can be demonstrated in infancy in the condition known as "mirasmus," in which a shockingly large percent of hospitalized, motherless infants waste away and die. In the middle years, when our apparatus is more developed and reality offers opportunity for adequate gratification, the death rate is proportionately low. Woolf, for example, as late as 1937 wrote (1984, p. 105): "I will not yield an inch or a fraction of an inch to nothingness, so long as something remains." In old age, on the other hand, when the body has had to give up many biological and ego satisfactions, when even stop-gap regressive pleasures such as being fed and nurtured have lost their magnetism, the individual silently and perhaps gratefully gives in to the last pull of all, the return to the inanimate.

The last few years of Virginia Woolf's life were characterized by ever-increasing deprivation, as bit by bit she lost everything she held dear. This chapter will describe her slide toward death, as she was forced by the exigencies of life to give up every source of pleasure that made existence worthwhile.

The symbolic loss of her mother through the defection of Vita as a lover; the estrangement between Virginia and Vanessa, and Virginia's lifelong defeat in the struggle for her affections; the lack of gratification through the loss of her lover; the daily deprivations brought about by the war; Virginia's terrible disappointment with Leonard which reenacted her early disenchantment with her father as well as her oedipal defeat; the repetition during the war years of the horrors of her adolescence when her mother, her half sister, her brother Thoby, and her father died; the fact that she lost her sublimation through the waning of her creative powers and thus lost her identity as a writer, in addition to losing her writing audience as a result of the war; her identification with the senile unproductive Leslie Stephen; the destruction of her books, papers, artwork, and many of her most cherished possessions: all of these losses culminated in her return, through a watery grave, to the uterine symbiosis with mother and the state of nonbeing that was the only source of gratification left to the destitute Virginia Woolf.

THE RETURN TO PARADISE

We have discussed in detail the history of Virginia's relationship to Julia Stephen, and how, as a very little child, she turned away from her mother in order to preserve her selfhood. In so doing, Virginia gave up a great deal; she sacrificed the sensuous, ecstatic pleasures with Mrs. Stephen, as well as the sense of togetherness with her mother that enables a normal child to grow up strong and secure. In Vita Sackville-West Virginia realized both aspects of her early mother. In spite of her idiosyncrasies, Vita gave Virginia physical love for almost a decade without interfering with her autonomy, and as a result served as a beacon for a new surge of development in Virginia. Even though the physical relationship ended, she was able to internalize the loving aspects of Vita's personality to make possible the continuation of the maturational process.

The physical deprivation suffered by Virginia at the ending of their love affair, however, was another story. When little Virginia turned away from her mother in infancy, she set in motion a lifetime of depression. The physical relationship with Vita restored to Virginia the early paradise she had experienced with her mother. Thus Virginia, "cured" of her sorest grief, remained relatively free of depression for years.

It is always interesting to observe which passages Woolf chose to eliminate in corrected versions of her work. In the first draft of *Between the Acts* (1983, p. 93), Woolf, who was reading Freud's *Beyond the Pleasure Principle* (1923), wrote that "what binds us to life are the bodily pleasures; that we are held tight to the tree, as an airman, by the physical pleasures; smoking; eating; drinking; and other pleasures, lodged in us so that the human race may continue, so that we are bound to the world, even when the world is upside down." When Vita cut off her sexual relationship with Virginia, the loss of gratification loosened the physical ties that bound Virginia to the world, and helped make it possible for her to kill herself.

After the ending of the sexual relationship between the two

women, their lives drifted apart, and their meetings and letters grew fewer and farther between. But the daily horror of the war matured Vita, in the sense that she began to realize what was important to her. As a result, the women were able to experience a rapprochement of sorts. Vita, finally recognizing her need for Virginia, wrote her on April 23, 1939 (DeSalvo & Leaska, 1985, p. 423): "I don't like being cut off from you, and am thus making an attempt to get into touch." And on April 24, 1940 (opus idem., p. 431): Vita expressed even more fully Virginia's importance to her when she wrote: "Thank you for . . . being so permanently loving towards me—Your friendship means so much to me—in fact it is one of the major things in my life." Four days later, Virginia joyfully began: "Oh Potto was so glad to huddle upon the rung [of Vita's love] again. . ." But then she continued with what I believe was a dire warning to Vita: ". . . isn't it a duty, in this frozen time, to meet as often as possible? so that even in the cold night watches, when all the skeletons clank, we may keep each other warm? . . . Please, dearest Vita, come visit soon. . ." This letter, in particular the reference to the clanking of skeletons, is an ominous sign of Virginia's plans to take her own life, should Vita not respond to her outcry.

A few months later, six months before Virginia committed suicide, she cried out once more to Vita, this time more emphatically than ever; "I've been in such a pelt that I couldn't write before. So now merely suggest, emphatically, Friday 16th . . . stay the night . . . no evasions . . . guns are being emplaced on the Banks. So do come before its all ablaze. . . ." But once again Vita did not appear. Preoccupied with the war, her castle, and her garden, she was unable to hear the warning. . .

VIRGINIA'S PREDICTIVE DREAM

Virginia's poignant outcry, and Vita's inability to hear her are further expressed in a seminal dream Virginia had less than ten months before she took her life. She wrote Vita in early May, 1940 (1980, p. 396): "What a dream I had of you! A cow flew over us and crushed your nose—It went black. I had tapioca pudding handy, and applied it. Horror and guilt both strongly present."

At the time of this dream, the lives of both women literally were in danger of being crushed from on high. Bombers flew overhead almost daily, and dropped their deadly loads on Rodmell, which was close to the front lines. Sometimes the bombs dropped close enough to shake the windows of Monk's House, the Woolfs' home; another time the raiders flew directly over the heads of Leonard and Virginia, forcing them to lie down in the grass under a tree to protect themselves. The feeling that life was a daily nightmare was not fully conscious to Virginia, who experienced an exaltation under the bombing which perhaps was the most ominous indication of her incipient psychosis. She suffered in her dream the true feelings of horror which she was unable to experience in her daily life. She wrote in her diary (1984, p. 231), "One is too numbed to think."

The blackness of Vita's crushed nose in the dream is also revealing, as color in a dream is often a prediction. Black is the color of mourning ("when all the skeletons clank"), and in this case the prognosis is ominous. Virginia predicts that the war will crush her, just as her sexual identity has been crushed by Vita's abandonment.

The symbolism used in the dream is also informative. Woolf uses two mother symbols, one, a cow, and the other, tapioca pudding. The cow destroys Vita; the tapioca restores her. This certainly was the psychology of Vita, whose mother, as you will recall, alternately destroyed and seduced her. But as every aspect of a dream also represents the dreamer, we can safely assume that Virginia's dream is telling her (and us) something about herself. Vita literally was a lifesaver during this wartime period of semi-starvation: she sent the Woolfs frequent gifts of food, such as butter, cream, and meat pies from her farm (hence another origin for the cow symbol in the dream). Although Vita was a "restorative tapioca," she also was a "bomb dropper" par excellence, beginning with the very first she dropped on Virginia— the news that the Nicolsons were going to Teheran. Virginia's dream predicts that their relationship, like the one with her mother, could not last, and that the daily regime of deprivation and horror under which she lived would not allow her to survive yet another psychological bomb.

The black color of Vita's nose in the dream also tells us that given Vita's history, as well as Virginia's experience with her own mother, Virginia knew that sexual disappointment was a virtual certainty. She had used the color black to indicate their dying sexuality in a letter to Vita as early as October 30, 1930 (1978, p. 240), when Virginia wrote that the loss of intimacy with Vita meant that "a black crust forms." In my view, the black of Vita's "nose" (the nose often is used in dreams as a phallic symbol) in particular represents Virginia's grief and anger at what she senses is the permanent loss of their sexual relationship. But the cure for annihilation anxiety is mothering. ("so that even in the cold night watches . . . we may keep each other warm"). So Virginia applies tapioca pudding to Vita's wound to cure her. In a reversal of roles, Virginia knows that Vita's love can cure *her,* just as the constant presence of her mother would have cured the toddler Virginia during the original rapprochement. Vita sensed this, too, and indicated so in the previously quoted letter (Chapter 4) in which she states that she would like to help Virginia integrate her various splits. After Virginia died Vita knew it too, for many years later she wrote her husband (DeSalvo & Leaska, 1985, p. 444): "I still think that I might have saved her if only I had been there and had known the state of mind she was getting into."

In Virginia's last letter to Vita, on March 22, 1941 (1980, p. 484), when Virginia ostensibly was talking about Vita's birds who, like Virginia, were dying of starvation, she asked: "Do they all die in an instant?" Her question suggests that she was planning to take her own life, and worried that her dying would be protracted. The dream further intimates that Vita was correct in her speculations to Harold, that she indeed knew somewhere the depth of Virginia's need for her, and that the joy inherent in the relationship could have kept alive. But, sadly enough, Vita was unable or unwilling to listen to her own inner voice, and Virginia's poignant cries fell on unhearing ears.

VANESSA IS NO HELP

As was discussed in Chapter 5, from childhood on, whenever Virginia was distressed or needed comfort, she turned to Vanessa as a mother substitute. Thus when Virginia lost Vita as a lover, Vanessa felt her sister's desperation, but in customary fashion withdrew from Virginia and was no support in her grief.

Again, in 1940, the year before her suicide, when Virginia was besieged with anguish from every side, the two quarreled over what seemed a trivial incident, but really was occasioned on Virginia's part by terrible jealousy of others for whom Vanessa cared. In *The Masochist Is the Leader* (1981, p. 384), I state that "when the sadist is most needed is precisely when he becomes most aware of his need to be separate, because he is threatened by the emergence of his own wish for engulfment." I believe that Vanessa's pull toward engulfment was particularly strong at this time because of the need to escape her unbearable pain of loss, in combination with the magnetic pull of Virginia's dreadful need. Vanessa was living in agonizing grief over the death of her son, a loss which makes Virginia's privations in frank existential terms seem incommensurable. Nevertheless, although Vanessa's self-absorption was understandable, she again had proved unavailable at Virginia's time of need. As a result Virginia withdrew from her sister in hurt and anger, a move that proved to be catastrophic. For this time the rift became a fatal one. The sisters remained estranged for the rest of Virginia's life.

Vanessa did not cause Virginia's illness. But neither did she help in Virginia's terminal struggle. Like Vita, Vanessa might have saved the life of Virginia Woolf. And like Vita, Vanessa failed Virginia and gave her one less reason to live.

LEONARD'S CONTRIBUTION

Virginia was able to integrate her feelings of love and hate for Vita, and therefore her mother; but I do not believe she ever came to terms with the emotions she had for Leonard. Despite the propaganda issued by the Woolf estate, and Virginia's protestations of marital happiness, the fact that she needed a homosexual love affair, her refusal to see Leonard during her manic outbreaks, and the content of many of her works cry out that the marriage was far from satisfactory.

In a few uncharacteristically revealing holographs, later to be largely revoked, entitled *Possible Poems* (1983, Appendix B, pp. 503–505), Woolf thrust aside her customary ambiguity to switch a subtle spotlight onto the final months with Leonard. "Where do I go," she asks, "to cast from my shoulders the many coloured coat? The coloured coat of day; and night's black coat?" "Hate and love, as usual, tore her asunder," says Isa about her husband (Woolf, 1983, unpaginated holograph, p. 553). "Love struck at her and hate," Isa had stated earlier (p. 502). This ambivalence is the very conflict discussed in Chapter 1, in which we demonstrated that the child Virginia failed to achieve one of the major tasks of the rapprochement phase, the ability to reconcile feelings of love and hate. Although she apparently was able to take this fateful step with Vita, and thereby put her conflict with her mother to rest, Virginia's writing indicates that she never was able to integrate her rage at Leonard with her love for him, just as she couldn't resolve her feelings for "that ole wretch, the dearest of creatures," her father.

This "fatal flaw" in Woolf's personality structure turned out to be literally such. Finding her antagonistic feelings intolerable, there was no escape from the pain of her ambivalence. As a result, she was driven to turn the full fury of her rage against herself to keep her love for Leonard intact. Finding no possible alternative to dealing with so massive an amount of rage, Woolf took the path carved out during her rapprochement phase, when she "chose" to love her mother and hate herself. Given her history, at this time of conflict and multi-deprivation, Woolf's answer to her question, "Where to fly? Down what draughty tunnels?" (1983, p. 503, unpaginated, undated holograph) could only be death itself. "Where the eyeless wind blows? . . . & there grows nothing for the eye: no rose . . . where no evening lets fall her mantle . . . nor sun rises; . . . immortal flowers; unblowing, not growing; and change is not. . ."

What are the causes of Woolf's hatred unto death? We know her relationship with Vita led to the resolution of unfulfilled symbiotic longings. If this supposition is correct, we have to look to another source of her later life despair. Subsequent paragraphs in *Pointz Hall* (1983, pp. 503–550) suggest deceptions from the past "buried so deep it has taken me a lifetime to rummage out from those old cupboards . . . what the past, its men and women, have laid on my back." I believe that Woolf was referring to the hypocrisies of her parents' marriage, and in particular to the emotional dishonesty of her father.

While Leslie Stephen's deceitfulness may well have fueled

the storehouse of rage Virginia hoarded for years, past fury alone cannot account for emotional catastrophe. Such episodes require a precipitating factor in the present life of the subject, as well as a past history. We must ask what it was in the present that lit the "match" that set off the "dynamite." I believe that the "match" was Leonard, who, in his evaluation of *The Years*, evoked memories of confusion and rage engendered by Stephen's duplicity in Virginia's childhood.

One of Leonard's greatest services was to be Virginia's "reader" for each book at its conclusion, the time she was consumed with doubts as to the value of her book, and particularly vulnerable to the criticism of the outside world. When Leonard said he liked a piece—and up to this point he had liked everything she had written—Virginia had absolute confidence in his honesty and was able to put her apprehensions to rest. But when she showed him *The Years* (1937), her next-to-the-last book with which she had had great difficulty, Leonard really did not care for it. He feared—correctly—that she would commit suicide if she knew the truth about his opinion. He lied, therefore and told her the book was an "extraordinary" achievement. Virginia really was not convinced at first, writing in her diary "I cannot bring myself to believe he is right" (1984, p. 30). With her customary manner of dealing with rage, she tried to talk herself into accepting his evaluation. But on the deepest level, she was *not* deceived. His lie brought back painful memories of dishonest Leslie Stephen. It shook her to the core—as Sir Leslie had done.

It is interesting that by the time Virginia had finished her biography, *Roger Fry* (1940), Leonard perhaps understood that she could not tolerate his deceit, and this time, one year before her death, told her the truth (1984, p. 271). He felt Virginia had chosen "the wrong method . . . merely analysis, not history. Austere repression. In fact dull to the outsider. All those dead quotations." "It was like being pecked by a very hard strong beak," Virginia wrote, using an analogy she had used in *To the Lighthouse* about Mr. Ramsay. Although Virginia wrote that she felt convinced of her failure on listening to Leonard's opinion, it seems to me she was not nearly as devastated by the criticism as by his covert rejection and deceitfulness on reading *The Years*.

One must feel some sympathy for Leonard. For all the years

of their marriage, Virginia had treated him as if his whole raison d'être was to perform as her adjunct. Within the confines of his character, he had nobly met this task. But one cannot help wondering whether such neediness as Virginia's could be met indefinitely by anyone. As stated in my paper, *The Masochist Is the Leader* (1981, p. 386), there frequently comes an instance when the underdog awakens to reality and belatedly seeks to rescue his selfhood. I have called this awakening the "masochistic upheaval." Such was the moment Leonard reached at this time. It was indeed unfortunate that Leonard's "moment of truth" came at the time of Virginia's greatest need.

As was discussed in Chapter 1, Virginia's defect in self-esteem left her unable to judge her own worth or that of her writing. Hence she had to rely on her husband, just as she had depended on her father for feedback. I believe that Virginia, perceptive as she was, understood that Leonard did not like *The Years*. His criticism confirmed her mother's poor opinion of Virginia's productions. His dishonesty confused and disoriented Virginia, much as her father's had. This dishonesty, and Leonard's possible unfaithfulness (to be discussed later in this chapter) seem to me the major precipitating factors that set off the ancient storehouse of rage that Virginia turned against herself.

An abject example of Woolf's self-destructiveness can be viewed in *The Years,* written when she already was despairing the loss of Vita as a lover. It is understandable that Leonard did not like *The Years*. Many other people have not liked it, either. Virginia herself called it "a deliberate failure." "My own lyric vein is to be satirised," Woolf stated (1953, p.104). "Everything mocked." According to Victoria Middleton (1977, p.170): "Woolf seeks to deceive us into believing this is a coherent fictional world. Instead of being such a world, with order and rules of its own, *The Years* is an anti-novel." Woolf deliberately eschewed her usual style in the book. Her intent, according to her diary (p. 218), was to *avoid* "beautiful writing." While a rhythmic style is usually Woolf's literary signature, even the rhythm in *The Years* is exaggerated. Her diary (1932–1935) reveals extremes of pessimism and optimism, suggesting a manic-depressive mood which is reflected in her fiction. Middleton suggests a manic overcast in which "the author's mind appears to be caught up by the sonorous sounds until meaning becomes of secondary importance." Of even greater significance, diagnostically, is Woolf's revelation in her diary (1953, p. 233) that she sought to break up her stylistic continuity through the use of thought-skipping and parentheses. De Selincourt (as quoted by Middleton (1977) p. 160) characterizes *The Years* as "a kaleidoscope of tiny cubes of experience, each containing an infinity of consciousness yet each inevitably isolated from the rest." Woolf's diary (1953, p. 184) intimates that she refrained from using the unifying principle that characterizes earlier novels such as *To the Lighthouse* and *The Waves*. A depressive mood permeates *The Years*. We are shown repeatedly that there is no hope for mankind, that the cycle of lives throughout the generations will simply repeat itself, that instead of growth and change the characters merely reenact their pasts. Woolf, herself, stated her intention in *The Years:* "The point is that I myself know why it's a failure, and that its failure is deliberate" (1953, p. 267).

She achieved this first by slashing out "two enormous chunks" of *The Years,* the book Leonard had prevaricated about, just as playwright La Trobe, in *Between the Acts,* when angry with her audience, had slashed her scene in the middle until "its lifeblood must ooze" (Leaska, 1983, p. 533). In my opinion, these truncated sections of *The Years,* later to be published as *The Pargiters* (Leaska, 1977), were the clearest and most illuminating parts of the book. Whatever Virginia's conscious rationale for attempting to destroy her creativity and her novel, *The Years,* to this clinician, appears to be a self-destructive effort to turn aggression against herself and her work, rather than against Leonard, her father, and the repressive world of men. The defense of splitting asunder her feelings of love and hate was only partially successful. Virginia's strident need for authenticity forced her forbidden rage back into consciousness in the form of an ominous symptom. For, in her madness, Virginia Woolf heard "voices."

It is fascinating that neither her biographies, diaries, nor written works betray the content of these voices, but in a shortly-to-be-discarded paragraph, Virginia allows us a brief glimpse into their character. For, just as *all delusions reflect the central conflict* of a tormented psyche, Virginia's voices spoke her inner truth, that Leonard did NOT believe *The Years* was "extraordinary." He, like her mother, apparently did not value Virginia's gift to the world; and his words, like those of her father, could not be trusted.

"Some say this, others say that," she scolds (1983, p. 504, unpaginated undated holograph). "But . . . none says what we believe, there's no voice that speaks fresh and strong . . . free from the echoes and vibrations of the old voices . . . always with corrupt murmurs, always with some clink of the baser sort, these voices merely stir the long hairs that grow in the conch of the ear and make strange music, mad music, jangled and broken sounds."

Virginia bitterly speaks of her rejection of the deceitful ones, as she writes of "refusing this guide and that [as she had refused to see Leonard during her 1914–1916 psychosis], for they are equally deluded . . . we who lack leaders, and have at last come to that place where the leaders are deserters . . . must carry on without listening to the frantic cries of those who shore up their unbelief by our credulity . . . So on, little donkey, then, patiently stumble, bearing whatever you can bear, carrying still the burden of memories and possessions bequeathed to the cradle . . . [what] all the voices . . . murmur in the night, and come when you lie looking at the stars among the apple trees; . . . by the voices that . . . murmur in marketplaces. . . . voices that are heard . . . on the sirens that blow up the river. . .; and the voice of brawling men and women in bye streets; and [voices that] also come singly, at night, when unable to sleep, the window is thrust open, and from the heart of London, some one cries."

Virginia's dissatisfaction with Leonard was corroborated two years after he had given Virginia his "evaluation" of *The Years*. At that time, she was rewriting *Lapin and Lapinova* (1949), the tale she had begun perhaps twenty years before. In her 22 November 1938 diary entry (1984, p. 189) Woolf stated that it required all her courage to add a passage to the story. Virginia followed this remark with a stray thought about Leonard—suggesting that the added passages in some manner referred to her husband. In addition, Woolf's choice of character names was fraught with significance. With so careful a writer nothing was left to coincidence. Therefore, it is likely that the initial L for Lapin and Lapinova was designed to refer to the first initial of her husband's name. In psychoanalysis, when one thought follows another, it is considered free association. In this light, we can appreciate why she had put the story aside for twenty years. In addition to her fear that Leonard would understand the origin of the story, Woolf was unable to finish it because she could not admit to herself that she knew how it would end.

In the published tale, as retold in Chapter 3, Rosalind and Ernest are a rather ordinary young couple, who lead somewhat stereotyped sexual roles. They concoct a *folie à deux* fantasy in which they are two rabbits named Lapin and Lapinova who are absolute rulers of the lagomorphic world. Rosalind reigned here as she could not in life, and had her staid and stolid Englishman literally eating lettuce out of her hand. When life got boring or difficult, she would turn to her fantasy kingdom. "Without that world, Rosalind wondered, could she have lived at all?" This retreat to the imaginary kingdom worked well enough for perhaps a year or two until Ernest tired of the "game."

Leonard and Virginia Woolf also wove a fantasy world, a literary world, an oedipal world where they reigned supreme as king and queen of Bloomsbury. But unlike Lapinova, the Woolfs were able to transform Virginia's fantasy into reality. Virginia was truly enthroned as the genius whom Leonard protected so that she could write freely. Leonard was cast in the less gratifying dual roles of the all-accepting mother of early infancy and the encouraging father of adolescence, who benevolently passed judgment on Virginia's productions and thus affirmed their value and hers. When Virginia pined for Vita or Vanessa, or longed for her parents, or was stung by the "slings and arrows" of friends and critics alike, a retreat to her encapsulated literary world, like the refuge of Lapinova, soothed and restored her to sanity and life. Leonard's role, however, was not merely less gratifying, but inherently impossible, ultimately. When he, like Lapin, tired of the "game" in which he was largely the subject of the "queen," he destroyed Virginia's refuge as well as her narcissim, just as he had punctured his mother's balloon in his own childhood. The truth behind his seemingly innocuous opinion of *The Years* proved a catastrophic loss to Virginia. First of all, she lost her best friend and mentor. Then the queen who had ruled Bloomsbury for 25 years was dethroned, which almost certainly brought back disastrous memories of Virginia's original oedipal defeat. And her helpmate of almost 30 years, "Mother Leonard," who could be relied upon to "take out the thorns," became unavailable. In his place was critical Leonard, reminiscent of the "cold bath," Leslie Stephen. As it was with Lapinova, this emotional loss was too much for Virginia to bear.

After Leonard's "defection," just before the publication of *The Years,* Virginia actually thought of herself as a rabbit. On March 1, 1937, she wrote in her diary (1984), "I looked at my eyes in the glass once and saw them as positively terrified. It's the 15th of March approaching [the date of the book's publication] I suppose—the dazzle of that head lamp on my poor little rabbit's body which keeps it dazed in the middle of the road." Rosalind the rabbit wondered if she could live without the wish-fulfillment supplied by her fantasy world. Virginia Woolf tried, and discovered she could not. "Is this death?" asks LaTrobe in Woolf's last book, "when illusion fails?" (1983, p. 403). Virginia answered the question by killing herself.

"By the truth we are undone," Virginia ominously prophesied in *Orlando* (p. 203). "Life is a dream. 'Tis waking that kills us. He who robs us of our dreams robs us of our life."

WAS LEONARD UNFAITHFUL?

Between the Acts (1941), which has been described as "the longest suicide letter in history," gives further food for thought about the last few years of the Woolf marriage and their possible effect on her suicide. The novel intimates that Virginia may have had an even stronger reason for her disillusionment with Leonard than his lack of enthusiasm for her later works. In *Between the Acts,* Giles, husband to Isa, has an affair with Mrs. Manresa, which leaves Isa in profound despair. Woolf's penchant for using autobiographical material in her books strongly hints that Leonard, too, was having an affair at that time, possibly with Trekkie (Marjorie Tulip Parsons). After Virginia's death she became his life companion, the person to whom he dedicated his book, *Beginning Again.* She was his executrix and a major beneficiary of his will (*Virginia Woolf Quarterly,* 1976, pp. 251–252). The content of *Between the Acts* gives rise to the suspicion that Leonard also had affairs before, telling Virginia they had no meaning. "She could feel the Manresa in his wake," said Isa of her husband, Giles. "She could hear in the dusk in their bedroom the usual explanation. It made no difference; his infidelity—but hers did" (Woolf, 1941, p. 110).

Given the sexless nature of the marriage, it does seem that, sooner or later, affairs would be inevitable. There was Vita, of course. Even so, Leonard's unfaithfulness would have been excruciating to so jealous a person as Virginia, who even found it unbearable that her sister cared for a friend. In such a situation, to paraphrase Isa, "It made no difference; her infidelity—but his did."

Virginia's bouts of panic at Leonard's frequent periods of lateness also suggest that Leonard had had previous affairs, as well. As early as 1917 Virginia wrote in her diary (1977, p. 75), "L. went on to meet Edgar for a mysterious interview, and I came home with my book . . . & I watch 3 fireballs glowing red hot." According to Arlow (Symposium on the Primal Scene, Biscayne Bay, February 1983), fire is a symbol frequently associated with the observation of parental intercourse. The "3 fireballs glowing red hot" suggest that Virginia was picturing, at least in her imagination, that Leonard was sexually involved with someone else.

Whatever happened previously, I believe that by the time Virginia was writing *Between the Acts,* Leonard had really fallen in love. Overcome with jealousy, anxiety, and rage, in her customary manner, Virginia split off her anger from consciousness and regressed to a mass of splintered selves (1941, p. 185) that led to insanity and death: "I am not (said one) in my perfect mind . . . Home? Where . . . the maiden faith is rudely strumpeted . . . Is that a dagger that I see before me? . . . Lady, I love till I die, leave thy chamber and come . . . Where the worm weaves its winding sheet. . ."

Virginia had much difficulty with this book and wrote at least three drafts. It is interesting that the first version is full of Isa's rage at her husband, Giles, a materialist who does not understand his wife. With each draft, Woolf deleted more and more of the rage, until the published version appears to be a different book. The fact that this marital failure occurs in her last work and was written with great conflict and numerous strike-outs, particularly about the wife's anger over her husband's affair, strongly implies that Virginia's difficulties with Leonard contributed heavily to her suicide.

On the other hand, Mrs. Manresa, the character who stands for Vita, is treated very differently. She is presented as sloppy, sensual, vulgar, and promiscuous. Despite her vanities and indulgences, however, Virginia portrays her as the book's most lovable character. This bears out earlier suppositions (Chapter 4) that at the end of her life Virginia had forgiven Vita's sexual abandonment and infidelities and had integrated love and hate into a comfortable, loving relationship.

It is Giles rather than Manresa who does not make out well. Virginia depended on her husband to help her depression at the conclusion of each of her books. Since Leonard lied to Virginia about his opinion of *The Years,* and informed her that he disliked *Roger Fry,* he no longer could serve her in that capacity. In the first draft of *Between the Acts,* it is interesting that Virginia included the comments of the wife, Isa, about her husband, Giles, only to delete them in later versions. "Of course disillusionment followed directly upon the glory of creation. And the one man to save her from it was Giles . . . the physical attributes of the savior were his. But he had turned. And she too turned. . . ."

In the next paragraph, Giles comes across a snake which is in the process of swallowing a toad. The snake was unable to swallow, to "give death to life." In the opinion of Kushen (1981), this symbol represents an "inverted birth," the longing of Virginia Woolf to return to the vast nothing from which she came, the wish to go back to the womb. For the opposite of birth is death. Virginia, like the toad, was "stuck," unable either to live or to take her own life. Giles (Leonard's) foot, which came down on the snake's head and squashed both creatures, made the final move which released the toad to its "inverted birth." This gives credence to the supposition that Leonard's crushing remarks and possible extramarital activities were destructive to his wife and thus struck the final blow that released Virginia from her "stuck" position and pointed her on the road to death. In her description of an actual scene she and Leonard saw of a snake devouring a toad (1982, p. 338), Virginia comments: "L. poked its tail: the snake was sick of the crushed toad, & I dreamt of men committing suicide and could see the body shooting through the water." That it was "men" and not Virginia who shoots through the water to death implies that unconsciously she already knew in 1935 that she would take her own life, but was not yet ready to face it. By the time Virginia was finishing *Between the Acts,* things had gotten much worse. Her nephew Julian and many friends had died, Hitler had invaded Austria, Poland, Norway, Denmark, Holland, and Belgium; England had declared war on Germany, the Battle of Britain had taken place, and Virginia had lived through the experience of daily air raids on Britain. She could master the deaths, the defection of Vanessa, the loss of Vita, and possibly even the bombs dropping over her head. What she could not tolerate was her disillusionment with Leonard, because she needed him to be able to function in her life and work, and because her rage set off the storehouse of anger at her father she had buried most of her life.

That this resuscitated anger continued to fester was evident as late as two months before her suicide, when Virginia wrote to her doctor, Octavia Wilberforce, in January, 1941: "This hand doesn't shake from book hugging but from rage . . . I cooked lunch: and the rice floored me. that's why I rage, and am consulting a cookery book." Leaska's interpretation of this letter is as follows (1983, pp. 461–2): "I lugged books . . . and hugged books . . . now I rage . . . I am so unfit for domestic life I cannot even cook . . . I rage . . . my hand is palsied . . . I cannot write . . . behind it all is my father." The one detail, only hinted at, is the very one she had already explicitly written in her diary years earlier: "Father's birthday . . . His life would have entirely ended mine . . . No writing, no books. . ."

The overwhelming force of this rage was the straw that broke the donkey's back, that dauntless little donkey who had struggled all of Virginia's life to overcome a burden too heavy to lift alone (Woolf, 1983, unpaginated undated holograph): "The last donkey in the long caravanserai, crossing the desert . . . Burdened with bales roughly bound with thongs . . . out of which my memories, my possessions; what the past, its men and women, have laid on my back; saying . . . rise up, little donkey, and go on your way, burdened, until the heels blister and the hoofs crack. But there's no lying down; or laying aside; nor forgetting. . ." With the support of Leonard and Vanessa, and the love of Vita, Virginia had been able to surmount the terrible problems bequeathed to her by the past. But without her support system, her cries of distress unanswered, Virginia became terribly tired. The deaths of her friends and the daily anxieties and deprivation of living during the war became an intolerable burden. Dissatisfied with her writing, as her father had been at the end of his life, Virginia's existence no longer contained enough pleasure to make living worthwhile. The valiant blistered and hoof-cracked little donkey no longer could find the strength to lift her burden; Virginia Woolf was ready to lie down and rest at last.

"Love and hate—", Woolf comments (p. 215) about Isa, who feels in rapid succession contempt for Giles, and admiration for his extraordinary handsomeness, "Love and hate—how they tore her asunder! Surely it was time someone invented a new plot. . ." Woolf invented a new plot by turning her hatred against herself until it reached the pitch of self-murder. Then she could deflect her rage at both her husband and her father, and preserve her love for Leonard to the point of greatest denial (1980, p. 486): "I want to tell you that you have given me complete happiness." This action ensured that her rage was disposed of forever, and that at last she could experience the ultimate state of Nirvana. Only then could she cease the relentless tearing asunder of her self.

THE DEPRIVATION OF THE WAR YEARS

Virginia's grief over the loss of Vita as a lover, her disappointment with Leonard, and Vanessa's failure once more to respond to Virginia's pain all took place against the backdrop of World War II.

The war years, rampant with death and destruction all about her, were full of horror and deprivation for Virginia Woolf. The relentlessness of daily tragedies ("Who will be killed tonight?" 1984, p. 300) must have been a repetition for her of the devastation experienced during her adolescence, when her mother, father, half sister Stella, and brother Thoby died.

The *Diagnostic and Statistical Manual of Mental Disorders* (3rd ed. rev.) (1987) (DSM-III-R), the official psychiatric manual for of the American Psychiatric Association on the diagnosis of mental and emotional illness, lists significant psychological stressors from one to seven in increasing order of the severity of their contribution to the development or exacerbation of a current disorder. It is interesting that the DSM-III-R records multiple family deaths as the most extreme catastrophic event that can happen during the life of an adolescent. This, understandably, seems the precipitating cause of Virginia's emotional breakdowns at that time. In like manner, the direct experience of war, with life in constant jeopardy, surely must be judged a similar catastrophe in the life of an adult. For Virginia Woolf, it was an even worse calamity than for most people. In addition to the trauma of the war against Hitler, and the fact that she was married to a Jew, many of those closest to her died about this time. In the last decade of her life, she lived through the deaths of Lytton Strachey, Roger Fry, her half brother George Duckworth, Francis Birrell, her nephew Julian, Ka Cox, Janet Case, Virginia's mother-in-law Marie Woolf, Dora Carrington, Ottoline Morrell, and her half sister Stella's husband, Jack Hills. Each death took a bit of Virginia with it. "How much of a piece with our friends . . . we are" she wrote after the deaths of Lytton Strachey and Dora Carrington: "It is thus we die when they die" (1980, p. 120). Thus, in the last few years of her life, Virginia reexperienced the multiple catastrophic stressors of her adolescence, as well as enduring the actual horrors of World War II along with the rest of her contemporaries.

In addition to these traumas, in her last months Virginia was able to see very little of the friends who remained. According to Kushen (1983, p. 216), war isolated them from each other, as each was "busy with the more immediate and pressing demands on time and energy created by the deprivations, emergencies and duties it imposed." Thus she was deprived of the support and companionship of those friends and loved ones still alive, as well as those who died.

It would seem that this social alienation made her more vulnerable to privation. In that last year, Virginia sacrificed three houses, art, and press to the bombing of London. "I want my books & chairs & carpets & beds," she poignantly wrote (1984, p. 331). "—How I worked to buy them—one by one—and the pictures." At that time, the horror of destruction was with her constantly. For an individual as unable to cope with aggression as Virginia Woolf, the constant destruction and the grief it caused surely was an open invitation to regression and psychosis.

All Virginia's ordinary everyday pleasures as well seemed to have been sapped by the war. Along with more catastrophic losses, even the simplest of "creature comforts" became war casualties. "Lord this is the worst of all my life's experiences," she wrote at another time that year (1984, pp. 234–235). . . . "Yes, it's an empty meaningless world now . . . This feeling is different from any before. And all the blood has been let out of common life. No movies or theatres allowed. No letters, except strays from America . . . No friends write or ring up . . . Of course all creative power is cut off."

Perhaps her greatest loss was the ability to write. Writing was Virginia Woolf's most important means of sublimating her unrequited yearnings, as well as pent-up rage. Its loss left her with an overwhelming degree of anger, the force of which, in customary fashion, she could only turn against herself. "If one cant write," she wrote, "one may as well kill oneself" (1984, p. 239).

Writing was also one of her primary means of binding anxiety and grief. "How am I to describe anxiety?" she wrote (1984, p. 125). "I've battened it down under this incessant writing . . . as I did in the summer after Julian's death." Even more important, writing gave Virginia her autonomy. When she could write, she needed Leonard less to help her cope with "the thorns" of daily living.

To one who had suffered an identity problem from early on, loss of self meant death itself. "The writing 'I' has vanished," she wrote, when the war threatened to curtail completely the sale of her books. "No audience. No echo. That's part of one's death" (1984, p. 293). Writing was one of her greatest pleasures, and for that reason the loss of her ability moved her a giant step further down the ladder to nonexistence. "Shall I ever write again one of those sentences that gives me intense pleasure?" she wrote (1984, p. 357). Her pessimism about recovering her talents was intensified by the frightening identification with her father, who at Virginia's age had permanently lost his ability to write. As early as 1921, when she was thirty-nine years old (1978, p. 142), she wrote, "When one leaves a life work at sixty one dies." As a result of unresolved symbiosis with her mother, fear of loss of self to father and mother both, profound disappointment with the three most important people in her life, Leonard, Vita, and Vanessa, the many deaths of friends and family, as well as her inability to write, then, the vulnerability of Virginia Woolf's personality structure was heightened by the catastrophic deprivations of the war. For the Virginia Woolf who had stated: "I will not yield . . . a fraction of an inch . . . to nothingness, so long as something remains" there was no recourse but to revert to that last remaining pleasure, nonexistence. The Death Instinct had finally triumphed over the mighty pull to life that had sustained Virginia Woolf for over fifty-nine years.

SUMMARY

In summary, then, if it truly be pleasure that binds us to life, holds us "tight to the tree, as an airman, . . . so that we are bound to the world, even when the world is upside down," Virginia Woolf's last few years, with their deprivation of all that gave life meaning, document a dizzying descent into death.

The first blow that strained much of the physical gratification from Virginia's existence was the loss of Vita Sackville-West as lover. Virginia had developed enough during the course of their relationship to enable her to maintain her love for Vita in spite of the deprivation; but the loss of sexual fulfillment erased a great deal of joy from Virginia's life. She not only forfeited the single source of sexual gratification she had known as an adult, but never again was able to climb the glorious peaks of creativity she had reached during the sexually active period of the relationship. The years of their romance marked the golden decade of Virginia's life. The pleasure experienced with Vita had returned Virginia to the paradise she shared with her mother, the "base upon which life stands." As with her mother, Vita proved truly irreplaceable. When Virginia lost her lover life began its downhill slide.

As she had done all their lives when she was in trouble, Virginia turned to her sister Vanessa for comfort. And as always, when Virginia approached Vanessa in desperation, a combination of fear of loss of autonomy and need for sadistic withdrawal made Vanessa unavailable. In the last year of Virginia's life, the sisters were estranged from each other, met only in the company of others, and wrote each other not at all until the week before Virginia killed herself. Vanessa's emotional unavailability, reminiscent of her mother's, deprived Virginia of an important source of comfort and pleasure at a time when only Vanessa conceivably could have made a difference. Thus she was an important motivating factor in Virginia's retreat to death.

Perhaps Virginia's greatest blow was the loss of faith in her husband. Leonard had served as a source of support for Virginia throughout most of their twenty-seven-year marriage. Not the least of his contributions was his ability to remove the mental "thorns" from Virginia's sensitive emotional "skin." In particular, he served as reader at the completion of each of her books, at a time when she was particularly vulnerable to criticism.

When Virginia finished *The Years,* an "anti-novel" greatly motivated by her need for self-destruction, Leonard disliked the book. Afraid that she would kill herself if he told her the truth, he lied and said it was "extraordinary." On an unconscious level, Virginia was not deceived. The discarded holographs of her last book, *Between the Acts,* are replete with disguised references to Leonard's deceitfulness, and suggest that her "voices" alone spoke the truth. When he read her biography, *Roger Fry,* a year before her death, Leonard, who perhaps understood what havoc his prevarication had caused, was openly critical. His words made Virginia feel she was a failure, but she was not as devastated as she had been by his deceitful "opinion" of *The Years.*

In *Between the Acts,* called "the longest suicide note in the English language," the hero Giles is unfaithful to Isa, his wife, as he had been many times before. As a result Isa wants to die. "O that our human pain could here have ending," she murmured (1941, p. 180). She is filled with rage at Giles in the first versions of the novel, but gradually tones down the anger until the last draft is actually a different novel. Given Woolf's penchant for incorporating autobiographical material into her novels, I believe that Leonard actually was unfaithful to Virginia, and that in the last years of her life formed an important alliance with another woman. Under these conditions, Virginia, like her heroine Isa, did not want to live. Contributing greatly to Virginia's wish to die was her inability to write. During the war years, the sale of Virginia's books all but disappeared. Without an audience, Virginia's hard-won identity, her "writing I," had vanished. In addition to the pleasure experienced in writing, she lost her major means of sublimating anger and grief, as well as her way of "battening down" anxiety.

The terrible emotional loss of the three most important people in her life, Vita, Leonard, and Vanessa, as well as Virginia's inability to write, took place against the backdrop of World War II. In the last five years of her life, Virginia lived through the deaths of many of her closest friends, as well as her beloved nephew, Julian. Toward the end, she lived in daily fear for her life in the frequent bombings of Rodmell. She suffered the destruction of her London homes as well as her most precious possessions. Even the most basic creature comforts, such as food and clothing, in great measure were taken away from her. At the end, every pleasure that bound her to earth was cut off, until only the return to the inanimate remained. For the valiant Virginia Woolf (1941, p. 297), "Against you I will fling myself, unvanquished and unyielding, O Death," the Death Instinct had finally triumphed.

Out the gate . . .

. . . over the downs . . .

. . . into the River Ouse . . . .

. . . where she floated gently downstream

Notes

[The numbers indicate the page on which the source is cited.]

INTRODUCTION
NOTES TO PAGES 15–19

15. Nicolson, Nigel. *Portrait of a Marriage* (London: Weidenfeld and Nicolson, 1973).
15. Woolf, Leonard. *The Journey Not the Arrival Matters* (New York and London: Harcourt, Brace, 1968).
15. Woolf, V. *The Diary of Virginia Woolf*, Vol. 5 (New York and London: HBJ, 1984).
15. Garnett, Angelica Bell. *Deceived with Kindness* (San Diego, New York and London: HBJ, 1985).
15. Kushen, Betty. *Virginia Woolf and the Nature of Communion* (West Orange, N.J.: Raynor Press, 1983.)
16. Leaska, Mitchell. *Pointz Hall* (New York: University Publications, 1983).
16. Woolf, V. *Between the Acts* (New York and London: Harcourt, Brace, 1941).
16. Woolf, V. *The Diary of Virginia Woolf*, Vol. 5 (New York and London: HBJ, 1984).
17. Woolf, V. *The Years* (New York and London: Harcourt, Brace, 1937).
17. Woolf, V. *A Writer's Diary* (New York and London: 1953).

18. Woolf, V. *Collected Essays,* Vol. 2 (New York and London: Harcourt, Brace, 1967).

18. Bell, Quentin. *Virginia Woolf, A Biography,* Vol. 2 (New York and London: HBJ, 1972).

18. Woolf, V. *The Letters of Virginia Woolf,* Vol. 3 (New York and London: HBJ, 1977).

18. Woolf, V. *The Letters of Virginia Woolf.* Vol. 6 (New York and London: HBJ, 1980).

CHAPTER 1

NOTES TO PAGES 21–29

21. Bell, Quentin. *Virginia Woolf, A Biography,* Volumes 1 and 2 (New York and London: HBJ, 1972).

21. Wolf, E., and Wolf, I. We perished each alone, a psychoanalytic commentary on Virginia Woolf's "To the Lighthouse". *International Review of Psychoanalysis,* Part 1, 6, 1979.

22. Rose, Phyllis. *A Woman of Letters, A Life of Virginia Woolf* (London: Oxford University Press, 1978). The phrase "The Invalid Lady of Bloomsbury" was coined by E. M. Forster in 1941.

22. Hinsie, Leland, and Campbell, Robert J. *Psychiatric Dictionary* (4th edition) (London and Toronto: Oxford University Press, 1977).

22. Woolf, V. *The Waves* (New York and London: HBJ, 1931).

22. Freud, Sigmund. *Mourning and Melancholia,* Standard Edition, Vol. 14 (1917).

22. Freud, Sigmund. *"Group Psychology and the Analysis of the Ego,* Standard Edition, Vol. 18 (1921).

23. Freud, Sigmund. *Abstracts of the Standard Edition of the Complete Psychological Works of Sigmund Freud* (New York: International Universities Press, 1973).

23. Freud, Sigmund. The dissection of the psychical personality. In *New Introductory Lectures on Psychoanalysis* (New York: W. W. Norton, 1933).

23. Greenacre, Phyllis. The childhood of the artist: Libidinal phase development and giftedness. *The Psychoanalytic Study of the Child,* Vol. 12 (1957).

23. Woolf, Virginia (Stephen). Virginia's first recorded letter, written at the age of six to her godfather, James Russell Lowell, reads: "My dear Godpapa have you been to the Adirondacks and have

you seen lots of wild beasts and a lot of birds in their nests you are a naughty man not to come here good bye your affect Virginia" (Bell, 1972, Vol. 1).

23. Jacobson, Edith. Contributions to the metapsychology of cyclothymic depression. In: *Affective Disorders*, Ed. P. Greenacre. (New York: International Universities Press, 1953).

23. Fieve, Ronald R. The lithium clinic. A new model for the delivery of psychiatric services. *American Journal of Psychiatry*, 1975, 132.

24. Mahler, Margaret, Pine, Fred, and Bergman, Anni. *Psychological Birth of the Human Infant* (New York: Basic Books, Inc., 1975). Margaret Mahler was the towering pioneer of separation individuation theory, the psychology of human symbiosis and its resolution. Without her herculean contributions, this chapter could not have been written. The following definitions of the various phases of separation individuation are taken from *The Psychological Birth of the Human Infant*, by Mahler, Pine, and Bergman:

Symbiosis: "That stage of undifferentiation, of fusion with mother, in which the 'I' is not yet differentiated from the 'not-I' and in which inside and outside are only gradually coming to be sensed as different" (p. 44).

Differentiation (the term used by Mahler for beginning separation from the mother): "The . . . infant has left the vague twilight state of symbiosis and has become more permanently alert and perceptive to the stimuli of his environment, rather than to his own bodily sensations, or to sensations emanating within the symbiotic orbit only . . . Total bodily dependence on mother begins to decrease as the maturation of locomotor partial functions brings about the first tentative moving away from her" (pp. 289–290).

Practicing: "The second subphase of separation-individuation, lasting from about 9 months to about 14 months of age. During this period the infant is able to actively move away from mother, and return to her, first by crawling and later by the mastery of upright locomotion. It is a period in which the exploration of the environment, animate and inanimate, and the practicing of locomotor skills are highly invested with lbidinal energy" (p. 291).

Rapprochement: "The third subphase of separation-individuation, lasting from 14 or 15 months to about 24 months of age and even beyond. [Mahler sometimes represents the end of this period as 30 months of age.] It is characterized by a rediscovery of mother, now a separate individual, and a returning to her after the obligatory forays of the practicing period . . . It often culminates in a more or less transient rapprochement crisis which is of great developmental significance" (pp. 291–292).

Object Constancy: "The task to be achieved in the course of the normal separation-individuation process is the establishment of both a measure of object constancy and a measure of self constancy, an enduring individuality, as it were" (p. 223).

24. Woolf, V. *Moments of Being* (New York and London: HBJ, 1976).
27. Woolf, V. *To the Lighthouse* New York and London: Harcourt, Brace, 1927).
27. Wolf, E., and Wolf, I. We perished each alone. *International Review of Psychoanalysis,* Part 1, 6, 1979.
27. Masterson, J., and Rinsley, D. The borderline syndrome; The role of the mother in the genesis and structuring of the borderline personality. *The International Journal of Psychoanalysis,* 1975, Vol. 56.
27. Kaplan, Louise. *Oneness and Separateness; From Infant to Individual* (New York: Simon and Schuster, 1978).
29. Roswell, Florence, and Natchez, Gladys. *Reading Disability—A Human Approach to Learning* (New York: Basic Books, 1979).

NOTES TO PAGES 29–35

30. Woolf, V. *The Waves* (New York and London; Harcourt, Brace, 1931).
30. Freud, Sigmund. *Neuroses and Psychoses,* SE, 10 (1924).
30. Freud, Sigmund. *The loss of reality in neurosis and psychosis,* SE, 10 (1924a).
30. Mahler, Margaret. "On the significance of the normal separation-individuation process, In: *Selected Papers of Margaret Mahler,* Vol. 2 (Jason Aronson, New York, 1965).
31. Freud, Sigmund. *Mourning and Melancholia,* SE, 14 (1917).
32. Garnett, Angelica. In: *Virginia Woolf, Miscellany,* No. 15 (Christmas, 1980).
33. Woolf, V. *The Waves* (New York and London: Harcourt, Brace, 1931).
33. Woolf, V. *The Letters of Virginia Woolf,* Vol. 1 (New York and London; HBJ, 1975).
33. Woolf, V. *Moments of Being* (New York and London: HBJ, 1976).
33. Woolf, V. *Flush* (New York and London: Harcourt Brace, 1933).
33. Woolf, Virginia (Stephen). The experiences of paterfamilias. In' *"Hyde Park Gate News,"* August 22, 1982, Vol ii, 32. Reprinted in *A Cockney's Family Experience and the Experience of a Paterfamilias,* Ed., Suzanne Henig (San Diego: San Diego State University Press, 1972).

34. Stephen, Adrian. On defining psychoanalysis. *British Journal of Medical Psychology,* 1931, 11.
34. Bibring, E. The mechanism of depression. In: *Affective Disorders,* Ed., P. Greenacre (New York: International Universities Press, 1954).
34. Freud, Sigmund. *Splitting of the ego in the process of defense,* SE, Vol. 23 (London: Hogarth Press, 1938).
34. Mahler, Margaret. Notes on the development of basic moods; the depressive affect. In: *Psychoanalysis—A General Psychology, Essays in Honor of Heinz Hartmann,* Ed. R. M. Loewenthal, L. M. Newman, R. M. Schur, and A. J. Solnit (New York: International Universities Press, 1966).
35. Freud, Anna. Aggression in relation to emotional development; normal and pathological. *The Psychoanalytic Study of the Child,* 1948, Vol. 3.

Notes to Pages 35–45

35. Mahler, Margaret, Pine, F., and Bergman, A. *The Psychological Birth of the Human Infant* (New York: Basic Books, 1975).
35. Meissner, W. W. *Internalization in Psychoanalysis* (New York: International Universities Press, 1981).
36. Bell, Quentin. *Virginia Woolf, A Biography,* Vol. 1 (New York and London: HBJ, 1972).
36. Jacobson, Edith. Normal and pathological moods; their nature and function. *The Psychoanalytic Study of the Child,* 1957, Vol. 12.
37. Freud, Sigmund. *Constructions in Analysis,* SE, 1937D, 23/260. Two of Freud's most famous cases, the "Rat Man" and the "Wolf Man," are examples of full-length constructions. The entire latter case revolves around one.
38. Woolf, V. *Moments of Being* (New York and London: Harcourt Brace, 1976).
38. Woolf, V. *A Writer's Diary* (New York and London: HBJ, 1954)
38. Woolf, V. *Between the Acts* (New York and London: Harcourt, Brace, 1941).
40. Pippett, A. *The Moth and the Star, A Biography of Virginia Woolf* (Boston and Toronto: Little, Brown and Co., 1953).
40. Woolf, V. *A Room of One's Own* (New York and London: Harcourt, Brace, 1929).
40. *New York Post,* Oct. 23, 1987. That things have not changed much from the "Oxbridge" days is suggested by the following discrimination against women practiced today by male New York clubs.

For example, at the Links Club on East 62nd Street, "women are barred from using the stairway because their heels catch on the carpet." Crain's New York Business informs us that "women can take the elevator, but they are barred from the main dining room, except on twice-weekly Ladies Nights." Women may not swim at the City Athletic Club at all "unless they want to swim nude with us," reported one member. And shades of Virginia Woolf!— "Women dining at the Knickerbocker Club have to eat with cheap flatware, while the real men members get sterling silver cutlery— polished daily—in the all-male dining room. The ladies get sugar cubes; the men have sterling sugar bowls."

41. Mahler, Margaret. On symbiotic child psychosis. In: *Selected Papers,* Vol. 1 (New York and London: Jason Aronson, 1979).
41. Bowlby, J. Grief and mourning in infancy and early childhood. *The Psychoanalytic Study of the Child,* 1960, Vol. 15.
41. Mahler, Margaret, Pine, Fred, and Bergman, Anni. *Psychological Birth of the Human Infant* (New York: Basic Books, 1975).
41. Woolf, V. *Night and Day* (New York and London: Harcourt, Brace, 1920).
41. Bell, Quentin. *Virginia Woolf, A Biography* (New York and London: Harcourt, Brace, 1972).
41. Mahler, Margaret. Notes on the Development of Basic Moods; The depressive affect. In: *Psychoanalysis—A General Psychology, Essay in Honor of Henry Hartmann,* Ed. R. M. Loewenthal L. M. Newman, R. M. Schur, & A. J. Solart. New York: International Universities Press, 1966.

CHAPTER 2
NOTES TO PAGES 46–52

46. Woolf, V. *To the Lighthouse* (New York and London: Harcourt, Brace, 1927).
46. Woolf, Virginia. *A Writer's Diary* (New York and London, Harcourt, Brace, 1954). Woolf planned *TTL* . . . "to have father's character done complete in it; and mother's; and St. Ives; and childhood; and all the usual things I try to put in—life, death, etc."
48. Bond, Alma H. Virginia Woolf—Manic-depressive psychosis and genius: An illustration of separation-individuation theory. *Journal of the American Academy of Psychoanalysis,* April 1985, Vol. 13, p. 2.
48. The American Psychiatric Association's *Psychiatric Glossary* (Washington, D. C.: American Psychiatric Press. Inc. 1984), defines

the Oedipus complex as the "Attachment of the child to the parent of the opposite sex, accompanied by envious and aggressive feelings toward the parent of the same sex."

48. Stephen, Leslie. *The Mausoleum Book.* Ed., Alan Bell (Oxford: Clarendon Press, 1977).

49. Kushen, Betty. "Virginia Woolf: Metaphor of the Inverted Birth." In *American Imago* (1981).

49. Woolf, Virginia. *Orlando* (New York and London: Harcourt, Brace, 1956).

49. Love, Jean O. *Virginia Woolf, Sources of Madness and Art* (Berkeley: University of California Press, 1977).

50. Hartmann, H., Kris, E., and Lowenstein, R. Notes on the theory of aggression. In *The Psychoanalytic Study of the Child,* Vol. III/IV (New York: International Universities Press. 1949). Hartmann, Kris, and Lowenstein speak of the conflict-free functions of the ego, which include creativity.

50. Woolf, V. *Night and Day* (New York: Harcourt, Brace, 1920).

50. Laing, R. D. *Sanity, Madness, and the Family* (New York: Basic Books, 1964).

52. Woolf, V. *A Room of One's Own* (New York and London: Harcourt, Brace, 1929).

52. Woolf, V. *Three Guineas* (New York and London: Harcourt, Brace, 1938).

52. Bell, Quentin. *Virginia Woolf, a Biography,* Vol. 2 (New York and London: HBJ, 1972).

52. Woolf, V. *To the Lighthouse* (New York and London: Harcourt, Brace, 1927).

Notes to Pages 53–59

53. Rose, Phyllis. *Woman of Letters, A Life of Virginia Woolf* (London: Oxford University Press. 1978).

53. Stephen, Leslie. *The Mausoleum Book* (Oxford: Clarendon Press. 1977).

55. Woolf, V. Old Bloomsbury (1921 or 1922). In *Moments of Being* (New York and London: HBJ, 1976).

55. Woolf, V. Collected Essays II, 1966, (New York and London: HBJ).

57. Woolf, V. *A Writer's Diary* (New York and London. HBJ, 1954).

58. Woolf, V. *The Letters of Virginia Woolf,* Vol. 1. 1888–1912 (New York and London: HBJ, 1975).

58. Woolf, V. *Mrs. Dalloway* (New York and London: Harcourt, Brace, 1925).

58. Bell, Vanessa. A Portrait of Virginia Woolf. An interview with Vanessa Bell, quoted on BBC (Houghton Library, Harvard University, Cambridge, Mass., 1956).

59. Annan, Noel. *Leslie Stephen, The Godless Victorian* (New York: Random House, 1984).

NOTES TO PAGES 60–64

60. Stephen, Leslie. *The Mausoleum Book* (Oxford: Clarendon Press, 1977).

60. Woolf, V. A Sketch of the Past. In *Moments of Being* (New York and London: HBJ, 1976).

61. Kennedy, Richard. *A Boy at the Hogarth Press* (San Diego, Calif: Aolean Press, 1972).

61. Woolf, Virginia. Leslie Stephen (1932). In *The Captain's Death Bed, and Other Essays* (New York and London: HBJ).

61. Bell, Quentin. *Virginia Woolf, A Biography*, Vol. 1 (New York and London, HBJ, 1972).

61. Herzog, J. M. On father hunger: The father's role in the modulation of the aggressive drive and fantasy. In *Father and Child*, (Boston: Little, Brown, 1982).

62. Woolf, V. *The Letters of Virginia Woolf*, Vol. 1 (New York and London: HBJ, 1975).

62. Rose, Phyllis. *Woman of Letters, A Life of Virginia Woolf* (London: Oxford University Press, 1978).

62. Woolf, V. *The Years* (New York and London: Harcourt, Brace, 1937).

62. Woolf, V. *Roger Fry: A Biography*. (New York and London: Harcourt, Brace, 1940).

63. Woolf, V. *Between the Acts* (New York and London: Harcourt, Brace, 1941).

63. Woolf, V. *The Letters of Virginia Woolf*, Vol. VI (New York and London, 1980).

64. Hill, Katherine C. *Virginia Woolf and Leslie Stephen: A Study in Mentoring and Literary Criticism* (New York: Columbia University, 1979).

NOTES TO PAGES 65–67

65. Spater, G., & Parsons, L. *A Marriage of True Minds* (New York & London: HBJ, 1977).

65. Love, Jean O. *Virginia Woolf, Sources of Madness and Art* (Berkeley: University of California Press, 1977).
65. Wolf, E., and Wolf, I. We perished each alone, a psychoanalytic commentary on Virginia Woolf's *To the Lighthouse* (In International Review of Psychoanalysis, Part 1, 6, 1979).
66. Annan, Noel. *Leslie Stephen, The Godless Victorian* (New York: Random House, 1984).
67. Blos, Peter. The second individuation process of adolescence. In *Psychoanalytic Study of the Child*, Vol. 22 (1967).

CHAPTER 3
NOTES TO PAGES 69–76

69. Woolf, V. *The Diary of Virginia Woolf*. Vol. 2 (New York and London: HBJ, 1978).
70. Ozick, Cynthia. *Art and Ardor* (New York: Alfred A. Knopf, 1983).
71. Spater, G. and Parsons, I. *A Marriage of True Minds* (New York and London: HBJ, 1977).
72. Woolf, Leonard. *Sowing* (New York and London: HBJ, 1960).
72. Garnett, Angelica. *Deceived With Kindness, A Bloomsbury Childhood* (San Diego, New York and London: HBJ, 1985).
73. Woolf, V. *The Diary of Virginia Woolf*, Vol. 4 (New York and London: HBJ, 1982).
73. Bell, Quentin. *Virginia Woolf, A Biography*, Vol. 2 (New York and London: HBJ, 1972).
74. Woolf, Leonard. *Downhill All the Way* (New York and London: HBJ, 1967).
75. Hinsie, L., & Campbell, R. *Psychiatric Dictionary* (Fourth Edition) (New York, London, and Toronto: Oxford University Press, 1977).
75. Woolf, V. *The Voyage Out* (New York and London: Harcourt, Brace, 1915).
76. Leaska, Mitchell A. The Death of Rachel Vinrace. In *The Bulletin of the New York Public Library*, Vol. 82, Number 3 (Autumn 1979).

NOTES TO PAGES 77–83

77. Bell, Quentin. *Virginia Woolf, A Biography*, Vol. 2 (New York and London: HBJ, 1972).
78. Ozick, Cynthia. *Art and Ardor* (New York: Alfred A. Knopf, 1983).
78. Spater, G., and Parsons, I. *A Marriage of True Minds* (New York and London: HBJ, 1977).

78. Woolf, V. *The Diary of Virginia,* Vol. 1 (New York and London: HBJ, 1977).
79. Woolf, V. *The Letters of Virginia Woolf,* Vol 1 (New York and London: HBJ, 1975).
80. Woolf, Leonard. *Sowing* (New York and London: HBJ, 1960).
80. Ozick, Cynthia. *Art and Ardor* (New York: Alfred A. Knopf, 1983).
80. Rose, Phyllis. *Woman of Letters* (New York: Oxford University Press, 1978).
80. Spater, G., and Parsons, I. *A Marriage of True Minds* (New York and London: HBJ, 1977).
80. Woolf, V. *Mrs. Dalloway* (New York and London: Harcourt, Brace, 1925).
81. Woolf, V. *Letters 3* (New York and London, HBJ, 1977).
81. Bell, Quentin. *Virginia Woolf, A Biography,* Vol. 2 (New York and London: HBJ, 1972).
81. Henig, Suzanne, *The Virginia Woolf Quarterly* (San Diego: 1973).
82. Woolf, V. *The Years* (New York and London: Harcourt, Brace).
83. Woolf, V. *The Voyage Out* (New York and London: Harcourt, Brace, 1915).

Notes to Pages 84–89

84. Bell, Quentin. *Virginia Woolf, A Biography,* Vol. 2 (New York and London: HBJ, 1972).
84. Woolf, Leonard. *Sowing* (New York and London: Harcourt, Brace, 1960).
84. Garnett, Angelica. *Deceived with Kindness* (San Diego, New York and London: HBJ, 1985).
86. Woolf, V. Lapin and Lapinova (1939). In *A Haunted House and Other Short Stories* (New York and London: HBJ, 1972).
87. Woolf, Leonard. *Beginning Again* (New York and London: HBJ, 1963).
87. Woolf, V. *The Diary of Virginia Woolf,* Vol. 1 (New York and London: HBJ, 1977).
87. Freud, Anna. *The Ego and the Mechanisms of Defense* (New York: International Universities Press, 1946). According to Anna Freud, denial consists of "the efforts of the infantile ego to avoid 'pain' by directly resisting external impressions" (p. 75). In Freud's case, "Little Hans" displaced his aggression and anxiety from his father onto horses, thus "denied reality by means of his phantasy." A. Freud comments that while this is considered normal in childhood,

if an individual attempts to avoid anxiety and neurosis by denying reality, the mechanism becomes overstrained. "If it happens in adult life," she states, "the ego's relations to reality will be profoundly shaken" (p. 87).

88. Spater, G., and Parsons, I. *A Marriage of True Minds* (New York and London: HBJ, 1977).

88. Woolf, V. *Orlando* (New York and London: Harcourt, 1928).

88. Bond, Alma H. The Masochist Is the Leader. *Journal of the American Academy of Psychoanalysis,* 1981, Vol. 9, No. 3.

88. Woolf, V. *Roger Fry, A Biography* (New York and London: Harcourt, Brace, 1940).

89. Woolf, V. (1921) *The Legacy* (published posthumously). In *A Haunted House and Other Short Stories* (New York: HBJ, 1972).

89. McCullough, David. *Book of the Month Club News* (1985).

NOTES TO PAGES 90–97

90. Woolf, V. *The Diary of Virginia Woolf,* Vol. 2 (New York and London: HBJ, 1977).

91. Freud, Sigmund. *Beyond the Pleasure Principle.* S. E. 1920G, Part 3 (1919). During the first month of life, the normal infant demonstrates an inborn unresponsiveness to external stimuli, known as the stimulus barrier. Some infants appear to be born without this physiological protection, and are overwhelmed by stimuli, with increased crying and other motor manifestations of discomfort.

91. Woolf, V. *The Diary of Virginia Woolf.* Vol. 1 (New York and London: HBJ, 1977).

92. Woolf, Leonard, *Downhill All the Way* (New York and London: HBJ, 1967).

92. Woolf, V. *The Letters of Virginia Woolf,* Vol. 1 (New York and London: HBJ, 1975).

92. Woolf, V. A Sketch of the Past. In *Moments of Being* (New York and London: HBJ, 1976).

93. Woolf, V. *A Room of One's Own* (New York and London: Harcourt, Brace, 1929).

93. Woolf, V. *Three Guineas* (New York and London: Harcourt, Brace, 1938).

93. Lilienfeld, Jane. Where the Spear Plants Grew. In *New Feminist Essays on Virginia Woolf* (Lincoln, Neb.: University of Nebraska Press, 1981).

93. Bell, Quentin. *Virginia Woolf, A Biography,* Vol. 2 (New York and London, HBJ, 1972).

94. Woolf, V. *The Diary of Virginia Woolf,* Vol. 1 (New York and London: HBJ, 1977).

95. . . . Woolf, V. A Summing Up (published posthumously). In *A Haunted House and Other Short Stories* (New York: Harcourt, Brace, 1949).

CHAPTER 4
NOTES TO PAGES 98–106

98. Bell, Quentin. *Virginia Woolf, A Biography,* Vol. 1 (New York and London: HBJ, 1972).

99. Woolf, Virginia. *The Letters of Virginia Woolf,* Vol. 1 (New York and London: HBJ, 1975).

99. Woolf, Virginia. *The Voyage Out* (New York and London: Harcourt, Brace, 1915).

102. Bell, Quentin. *Virginia Woolf, A Biography,* Vol. 2 (New York and London: HBJ, 1972).

102. Woolf, V. *The Diaries of Virginia Woolf,* Vol. 2 (New York and London: HBJ, 1976).

102. Kushen, Betty. *Virginia Woolf and the Nature of Communion* (West Orange, New Jersey: Raynor Press, 1983).

103. Woolf, V. *The Letters of Virginia Woolf,* Vol. 6 (New York and London: HBJ, 1980).

106. Woolf, V. *The Letters of Virginia Woolf,* Vol. 2 (New York and London: HBJ, 1976).

NOTES TO PAGES 106–112

106. Woolf, V. *The Diary of Virginia Woolf,* Vol. 1 (New York and London: HBJ, 1977).

107. Freud, Sigmund. *Beyond the Pleasure Principle,* S.E. 1920G, Part 3 (1919).

108. Bell, Quentin. *Virginia Woolf, A Biography,* Vol. 1 (New York and London: HBJ, 1972).

108. Woolf, V. *The Waves* (New York and London: HBJ, 1931).

108. Garnett, Angelica. *Deceived with Kindness* (San Diego, New York and London: HBJ, 1985).

109. Kushen, Betty. *Virginia Woolf and the Nature of Communion* (West Orange, New Jersey: Raynor Press, 1983).

109. Bond, Alma H. The Masochist Is the Leader, *Journal of the American Academy of Psychoanalysis,* 1981, vol. 9, no. 3.
110. Woolf, *The Waves* (New York and London: Harcourt, Brace, 1931).
111. Woolf, V. *Mrs. Dalloway* (New York and London: Harcourt, Brace, 1925).
111. Bell, Quentin. *Virginia Woolf, A Biography,* Vol. 2 (New York and London: 1972).
111. Spalding, Frances. *Vanessa Bell* (New Haven and New York: Ticknor and Fields, 1983).
112. Woolf, V. *The Letters of Virginia Woolf,* Vol. 1 (New York and London: HBJ, 1975).
112. Kushen, Betty. *Virginia Woolf and the Nature of Communion* (West Orange, New Jersey: Raynor Press, 1983).
112. Shainess, Natalie. *Sweet Suffering* (Indianapolis and New York: Bobbs-Merrill Co., 1984).

NOTES TO PAGES 113–116

113. Woolf, V. *The Waves* (New York and London: Harcourt, Brace, 1931).
113. Bell, Quentin. *Virginia Woolf, A Biography,* Vol. 1 (New York and London: HBJ, 1972).
114. Bond, Alma H. "The Masochist is the Leader," *Journal of the American Academy of Psychoanalysis,* Vol. 9, No. 3, 1981.
115. Woolf, V. *The Voyage Out* (New York and London: Harcourt, Brace, 1915).
115. Woolf, V. *Night and Day* (New York and London: Harcourt Brace, 1919).
115. Woolf, V. *Jacob's Room* (New York and London: Harcourt, Brace, 1919).
115. Woolf, V. *Mrs. Dalloway* (New York and London: Harcourt, Brace, 1925).
115. Woolf, V. *To the Lighthouse* (New York and London: Harcourt, Brace, 1927).
115. Woolf, V. *A Room of One's Own* (New York and London: Harcourt, Brace, 1929).
115. Woolf, V. *The Waves* (New York and London: Harcourt, Brace, 1931).
116. Woolf, V. *The Letters of Virginia Woolf,* Vol. 1 (New York and London: HBJ, 1977).

CHAPTER 5
NOTES TO PAGES 118–125

118. Woolf, V. *The Diary of Virginia Woolf*, Vol. 4 (New York and London: HBJ, 1982).

119. Freud, Sigmund *Beyond the Pleasure Principle* (New York, SE, 1920).

119. Woolf, V. *To the Lighthouse* (New York and London: Harcourt, Brace, 1927).

119. Woolf, V. *The Waves* (New York and London: Harcourt Brace, 1931).

119. Woolf, V. *Orlando* (New York and London: Harcourt, Brace, 1928).

120. Woolf, V. *The Diary of Virginia Woolf*, Vol. 2 (New York and London: HBJ, 1978).

121. Woolf, V. *The Diary of Virginia Woolf*, Vol.1 (New York and London: HBJ, 1977).

121. Woolf, V. *Monday or Tuesday* (New York and London: Harcourt, Brace, 1921).

121. Woolf, V. *Jacob's Room* (New York and London, Harcourt, Brace, 1922).

122. Bond, Alma H. The Masochist Is the Leader. *Journal of the American Academy of Psychoanalysis,* 1981, vol. 9, No. 3, 375–389.

123. Glendinning, Victoria. *Vita, The Life of V. Sackville-West* (New York: Alfred A. Knopf, 1983).

123. Nicolson, Nigel. *Portrait of a Marriage* (London: Weidenfeld and Nicolson, 1973).

125. Deutsch, Helene. Some forms of emotional disturbances and their relationship to Schizophrenia. *Psychoanalytic Quarterly,* 1942, vol. 2.

125. DeSalvo, Louise, and Leaska, Mitchell A. *The Letters of Vita Sackville-West to Virginia Woolf* (New York: William Morrow and Co., 1985).

125. Winnicott, D.W. *Collected Papers* (New York: Basic Books, Inc., 1958).

NOTES TO PAGES 125–139

125. Nicolson, Nigel, *Portrait of a Marriage* (London: Weidenfeld and Nicolson, 1973).

127. Glendinning, Victoria. *Vita, The Life of Vita Sackville-West* (New York: Knopf, 1983).

130. Sackville-West, Vita. *Behind the Mask* (1910, unpublished work).

131. Sackville-West, Vita. *Grey Wethers* (London: Heinemann, 1923).

133. Woolf, V. *The Diary of Virginia Woolf,* Vol. 3 (New York and London: HBJ, 1980).

133. Glendinning, Victoria. *Vita, The Life of Vita Sackville-West* (New York: Knopf, 1983).

133. Nicolson, Nigel. *Portrait of a Marriage* (London: Weidenfeld and Nicolson, 1973).

133. Bell, Quentin. *Virginia Woolf, A Biography,* Vol. 1, 1972.

134. DeSalvo, L., & Leaska, M. *The Letters of Vita Sackville-West to Virginia Woolf* (New York: William Morrow, 1985).

137. Sackville-West, V. *Seducers in Ecuador* (London: Hogarth Press, 1924).

138. Sackville-West, V. *The Land* (London: Heinemann, 1926).

139. Woolf, Virginia. *The Diary of Virginia Woolf,* Vol. 2 (New York and London: HBJ, 1978).

139. Sackville-West, V. *Passage to Teheran* (London: Hogarth Press, 1926).

NOTES TO PAGES 139–145

139. Woolf, V. *The Letters of Virginia Woolf,* Vol. 3 (New York and London: HBJ, 1977).

140. Woolf, V. *Mrs. Dalloway* (New York and London: HBJ, 1925).

140. Freud, Sigmund. *Beyond the Pleasure Principle,* S.E. 1920G, 1923.

140. Woolf, V. *The Letters of Virginia Woolf,* Vol. 3, 1977.

140. DeSalvo, L., and Leaska, Mitchell. *The Letters of Vita Sackville-West to Virginia Woolf* (New York: William Morrow, 1985).

141. The transference in psychoanalysis refers to that state in which the patient unconsciously relates to the psychoanalyst as to a significant figure from the past.

142. Woolf, V. *The Diary of Virginia Woolf,* Vol. 2 (New York and London: HBJ, 1978).

143. Woolf, V. *Orlando* (New York and London: Harcourt, Brace, 1928).

143. Woolf, V. *The Letters of Virginia Woolf,* Vol. 6 (New York and London: HBJ, 1980).

144. Kaplan, Louise. *Oneness and Separateness* (New York: Simon and Schuster, 1978).

144. Ray, Margaret H. Phenomenology of Failed Object Constancy. In

Self and Object Constancy, Ed. Lax, R., Bach, S., and Burland, J. (New York and London: Guilford Press, 1986).

145. Woolf, V. *To the Lighthouse* (New York and London, Harcourt, Brace, 1927).

145. Woolf, V. *The Waves* (New York and London: Harcourt, Brace, 1931).

145. Woolf, V. *Orlando* (New York and London: Harcourt, Brace, 1928).

145. Neugebauer, Roda. *The Creative Process in Relation to the Theme of Union and Separateness* (unpublished paper, 1986).

145. Woolf, V. *The Years* (New York and London: Harcourt, Brace, 1937).

145. Woolf, V. *Three Guineas* (New York and London: Harcourt, Brace, 1938).

145. Woolf, V. *Roger Fry: A Biography* (New York and London: Harcourt, Brace, 1940).

Notes to Pages 145–149

145. Bell, Quentin. *Virginia Woolf, A Biography.* V. 2 (New York and London: HBJ, 1972).

146. Glendinning, Victoria. *Vita, The Life of Vita Sackville-West* (New York: Knopf, 1983).

146. Moore, Madeline. *The Short Season Between Two Silences* (Boston, London, and Sydney, 1984).

146. Woolf, V. *Orlando* (New York & London: Harcourt, Brace, 1956).

146. Woolf, V. *The Letters of Virginia Woolf.* Vol. 3 (New York and London: HBJ, 1977).

147. Woolf, V. *The Letters of Virginia Woolf.* Vol. 6 (New York and London: HBJ, 1978).

148. Woolf, Virginia. *The Letters of Virginia Woolf.* Vol. 5 (New York and London: HBJ, 1979).

149. Woolf, Virginia. *The Letters of Virginia Woolf.* Vol. 6 (New York and London: HBJ, 1980).

Chapter 6
Notes to Pages 151–158

151. Freud, Sigmund. *Beyond the Pleasure Principle,* 1922 (Hogarth Press, London, 1948).

152. Woolf, V. *The Diary of Virginia Woolf,* Vol. 5 (HBJ, San Diego, New York and London, 1984).

156. Woolf, V. *Pointz Hall*. Mitchell A. Leaska, Ed. (University Publications, New York, 1983).

156. DeSalvo, Louise, and Leaska, Mitchell A. *The Letters of Vita Sackville-West to Virginia Woolf* (William Morrow and Co., New York, 1985.)

157. Bond, A. The Masochist is the Leader (New York: John Wiley and Sons, 1981).

158. Woolf, V. *The Letters of Virginia Woolf*, Vol. 6 (Harcourt Brace Jovanovitch, New York and London, 1980).

158. Woolf, V. *The Letters of Virginia Woolf*, Vol. 4 (New York and London, 1978).

158. Woolf, V. *Pointz Hall*, Ed. Mitchell A. Leaska (New York: University Press, 1983).

NOTES TO PAGES 159–162

159. Woolf, V. *The Years* (New York and London: Harcourt, Brace, 1937).

159. Woolf, V. *The Diary of Virginia Woolf*, Vol. 5 (San Diego, New York and London: HBJ, 1984).

160. Bond, A. *The Masochist is the Leader* (New York: John Wiley and Sons, 1981).

160. Woolf, V. *Roger Fry, A Biography* (New York and London: Harcourt, Brace, 1940).

161. Woolf, V. *A Writer's Diary* (New York and London: Harcourt, Brace, 1953).

161. Middleton, Victoria S. *A Deliberate Failure. Bulletin of the New York Public Library*, Winter 1977, Vol. 80 2.

161. Woolf, V. *The Diary of Virginia Woolf*, Vol. 4, 1982.

161. Woolf, V. *Pointz Hall*. Ed, Mitchell A. Leaska (New York: University Press, 1983).

161. Leaska, Mitchell A. Virginia Woolf, the Pargiter: A Reading of "The Years," *Bulletin of the New York Public Library*, Vol. 80, 2 (Winter 1977).

162. Woolf, V. Lapin and Lapinova. In *A Haunted House and Other Short Stories* (New York and London: Harcourt, Brace, 1949).

NOTES TO PAGES 164–167

164. Woolf, V. *Between the Acts* (New York and London: Harcourt, Brace, 1941).

164. Woolf, Leonard. *Beginning Again* (New York and London: Harcourt, Brace, 1963).
164. Leonard Woolf's Will with Notes by Beatrice Harrington. *Virginia Woolf Quarterly* (Aeolian Press, Vol. 11, 3–4, Summer and Fall 1976).
165. Woolf, V. *The Diary of Virginia Woolf,* Vol. 1 (New York and London: HBJ, 1977).
166. Arlow, Jacob. *The Primal Scene.* Symposium, Biscayne Bay, Fla., Feb., 1983.
166. Kushen, Betty. Virginia Woolf: Metaphor of the Inverted Birth. *American Image,* 38, 3, 1981.
167. Woolf, V. *Pointz Hall.* Ed. Mitchell A. Leaska (University Press, New York, 1983).
167. Woolf, V. *The Diary of Virginia Woolf,* Vol. 3 (HBJ, New York and London: 1980).

NOTES PAGES 167–173

167. Woolf, V. *The Diary of Virginia Woolf,* Vol. 5 (San Diego, New York and London: HBJ, 1984).
168. *The Diagnostic and Statistical Manual of Mental Disorders* (DSM-III) (American Psychiatric Association, Washington, D.C., 1980).
169. Woolf, V. *The Diary of Virginia Woolf,* Vol. 3 (New York and London: HBJ, 1980).
169. Kushen, Betty. *Virginia Woolf and the Nature of Communion* (West Orange, New Jersey: Raynor Press, 1983).
169. Woolf, V. *The Diary of Virginia Woolf,* Vol. 5 (San Diego, New York and London: HBJ, 1984).
170. Woolf, V. *Between the Acts* (New York and London: Harcourt, Brace, 1941).
170. Woolf, V. *The Diary of Virginia Woolf,* Vol. 2 (New York and London: HBJ, 1978).
173. Woolf, *The Waves* (New York and London: Harcourt, Brace, 1931).

Index